Praise for *The Hidden History of Guns and the Second Amendment*

"If every American were to read this book and take its message to heart, the lies that are used to divide could lose their power. And we might just find the common ground that so frequently eludes us."

—John Nichols, National Affairs Correspondent, *The Nation*

"America, with 5 percent of the population, ended up with 50 percent of all the guns, worldwide, in civilian hands."

—Medea Benjamin, author and cofounder of CODEPINK

"Thom is the professor America needs. If people knew what he knows, we'd have a vastly different country."

—Cenk Uygur, Host, *The Young Turks*, and CEO, TYT Network

"Hartmann unravels the anemic underpinnings of the deafening claims by gun rights advocates for constitutional sanction while showing how gun rights ideology, born from slavery, is rooted in racial hatred and tribalism manipulated by economic demands of racketeering gun manufacturers and their corporate and political allies."

—Robert F. Kennedy, Jr.

"When Thom Hartmann talks, I listen. This book about the history of guns in America is important, mind-opening, and profoundly helpful."

—Marianne Williamson

"Thom tells us what we can d̶ right now to move forward."

—Larry Cohen, Chair, Our Re
**Communications Workers **
Democracy Initiative

"Thom Hartmann adroitly links the relationship of guns to slavery from Columbus through Reconstruction to racism in present-day America. This book should be required reading for every legislator."

—Earl Katz, political ethicist and Emmy-nominated documentary producer

"A powerful stepping-stone to a new understanding about and approach to gun reform in the Wild West of nations."

—Mark Karlin, founder of BuzzFlash.com and former Chairman and President, Illinois Council Against Handgun Violence

"This profoundly personal yet insightful historical work so wonderfully encapsulates the pulse of our time and the sea change the Parkland kids and others have made in our national, and deadly, struggle with guns in America."

—Stephanie Miller, national radio host

"Political sloganeering aside, guns do in fact kill people. It's a national plague directly traceable to a handful of corporate profiteers, gun lobby extremists, and gutless politicians. In this liberating book, Thom Hartmann exposes their scam and proposes a path to gun sanity."

—Jim Hightower, populist radio commentator, syndicated columnist, and editor of the monthly newsletter *The Hightower Lowdown*

"There is a widely accepted false choice that either we protect the lives of our schoolchildren or we protect our freedom to own guns, but we can't do both. This book explains how we've come to think in such black-and-white terms and how the debate over guns has become so polarized as to seem intractable."

—John Robbins, bestselling author and cofounder and President, Food Revolution Network

THE
HIDDEN
HISTORY
OF GUNS *AND THE*
SECOND AMENDMENT

THOM HARTMANN

Berrett–Koehler Publishers, Inc.

Berrett-Koehler Publishers, Inc.
1333 Broadway, Suite 1000
Oakland, CA 94612-1921
Tel: (510) 817-2277
Fax: (510) 817-2278
www.bkconnection.com

ORDERING INFORMATION
Quantity sales. Special discounts are available on quantity purchases by corporations, associations, and others. For details, contact the "Special Sales Department" at the Berrett-Koehler address above.
Individual sales. Berrett-Koehler publications are available through most bookstores. They can also be ordered directly from Berrett-Koehler: Tel: (800) 929-2929; Fax: (802) 864-7626; www.bkconnection.com.
Orders for college textbook / course adoption use. Please contact Berrett-Koehler: Tel: (800) 929-2929; Fax: (802) 864-7626.

Distributed to the U.S. trade and internationally by Penguin Random House Publisher Services.

Berrett-Koehler and the BK logo are registered trademarks of Berrett-Koehler Publishers, Inc.

Printed in the United States of America

Berrett-Koehler books are printed on long-lasting acid-free paper. When it is available, we choose paper that has been manufactured by environmentally responsible processes. These may include using trees grown in sustainable forests, incorporating recycled paper, minimizing chlorine in bleaching, or recycling the energy produced at the paper mill.

Library of Congress Cataloging-in-Publication Data
Names: Hartmann, Thom, 1951– author.
Title: The hidden history of guns and the Second Amendment / Thom Hartmann.
Description: Oakland, CA : Berrett-Koehler Publishers, 2019. | Series: The
    Thom Hartmann hidden history series
Identifiers: LCCN 2018057773 | ISBN 9781523085996 (paperback)
Subjects: LCSH: Firearms—Law and legislation—United States—History. |
    United States. Constitution. 2nd Amendment—History. | Gun control—United
    States—History. | National Rifle Association of America. | BISAC: LAW /
    Constitutional. | HISTORY / United States / General. | SOCIAL SCIENCE /
    Violence in Society.
Classification: LCC KF3941 .H39 2019 | DDC 344.7305/33—dc23
LC record available at https://lccn.loc.gov/2018057773

First Edition
27 26 25 24 23 22 21 20 19   10 9 8 7 6 5 4 3 2 1

Book production: Linda Jupiter Productions; *Editor:* Elissa Rabellino;
Cover design: Wes Youssi, M.80 Design; *Text design:* Morning Hullinger, The Color Mill;
Proofread: Mary Kanable; *Index:* Paula C. Durbin-Westby

To the memory of my friend
Clark Stinson

CONTENTS

FOREWORD

By Mike Farrell

Years ago, probably the late '70s, I went to a fund-raising event in Los Angeles to hear Rev. George Regas, one of the founders of the Interfaith Center to Reverse the Arms Race. I remember being struck by a unique part of his fund-raising pitch that day. He said that our society's priorities are upside down: human existence is being endangered by the makers of war, so in a rational society those working for peace should be funded by the government while the Pentagon has bake sales to raise its budget.

He said it better than that, but the idea stuck with me. And when I think about it, so many of the things we do in this country tell me he's right. The "official" policies are too often counterproductive in a society that claims to respect the dignity of each individual, in a state that claims to believe in equality and says it intends to "promote the general welfare." The general welfare means, roughly, taking care of the needs of the common citizen. And that's us, folks.

But take a look at poverty, climate change, health care, racial and gender equity, the proliferation of guns; name your issue. Whatever it is, we clearly seem to have gone pretty far off track in a lot of areas in a lot of ways and find ourselves wondering why we're stuck in opposition to one another.

When that happens, I've found it helpful to look for thoughtful, clear-eyed people who are capable of taking a dispassionate look at a troubling issue or situation and parse it, take it apart logically, and in so doing provide a better understanding of not only the issue itself but its history, the factors or elements that have led us to a place that is so obviously deeply wrong but somehow seems too overwhelmingly complicated to ever get right.

Happily, there are such people in our world. They are leaders, but not necessarily part of formal leadership. Think of them as thought leaders. One of the best of them, I believe, is Thom Hartmann, the author of this book.

Like Rev. Regas, Thom recognizes that we have inverted our priorities and wants to do something about putting us back on our feet. Thom does it by first educating himself, and then reading more, debating, learning, studying, assessing, questioning, and challenging. Once his ideas are formed, he puts them out there by talking, speaking formally, broadcasting, studying more, challenging more, and writing. His books, more than 20 by now, cover a wide range of subject areas. But you've picked up this one because it deals with a very current, very deadly national dilemma: gun violence.

Typical of Thom, he doesn't simply leap into today's debate and make a well-thought-out argument on one side of a thorny question. Instead, in *The Hidden History of Guns and the Second Amendment*, he lays out a path of paving stones, asking you to look at the way in which firearms were introduced into our world, by whom, and for what. He walks you through a history replete with the ugliness of the worst kind of human behavior and allows you to see the processes by which a culture within a culture can develop. He explores racial attitudes, the extremes of colonialism, the demands of exploration, national expansion, and the costs of the assumption of white supremacy.

Much of what he relates about the development of our country will make you wince. But all of it is presented without fear or favor in order to create an understanding of who we are and how we came to the place we find ourselves in today.

And then he offers insights and ideas about what might be done to ease the pain, to find a way to resolve the apparent dilemma posed by the tension between those wanting to live a completely free and independent life and those living happily and productively in a free society that imposes necessary constraints. He points us toward finding a way to resolve it all in a manner that allows those with differing philosophies to respect themselves and one another, while living comfortably together.

Enjoy the trip. I did.

Mike Farrell, best known for playing Capt. B.J. Hunnicutt on M*A*S*H, *is the author of* Just Call Me Mike: A Journey to Actor and Activist *and* Of Mule and Man.

PREFACE

The characters I've played, especially Bret Maverick and Jim Rockford, almost never use a gun, and they always try to use their wits instead of their fists.

—James Garner

There was a high deck of wispy clouds, with bits of bright blue sky cracking through, and it was bitterly cold, two days before Christmas 2008, in Lansing, Michigan. The wind cut right through you. A little less than a foot of crystal-white snow covered the ground, most of it accumulated over a few small storms during the past two weeks.

Two of my brothers, one of their kids, and one of mine all drove out to the small nearby town of Mason, where one of the area's larger shooting ranges was located. My brother Steve has collected guns for years and even built a small shooting range behind his rural house on the Grand River. When my wife, Louise, and I visit Michigan, we usually stay with Steve and his wife, and during the summers we target-shoot competitively on his backyard range. (Steve is not a hunter; he's mostly a vegetarian, in fact.)

Inside the shooting range, there were numerous paper targets for sale; they included black-outlined Muslim men in turbans, depictions of big men with nappy hair, and the usual round bull's-eyes.

The store attached to the range was huge—from the outside it looked like a one-story warehouse with a few windows clustered around a bumped-out entrance with weather doors in the center of the long building. Inside, long rows of glass cases held many of the more than 2,000 guns they boasted of having in inventory.

Behind the glass cases were long stretches of shelves for ammunition, which I was pretty sure from previous visits were usually full. Today they were nearly empty.

I rented a .40 caliber semiautomatic pistol (wanting some practice with something that could kick) while my brothers and our kids were making their selections. The guy taking my money was tall and thin, his pale skin highlighted by wispy facial hair.

"I'll take two boxes of 40s," I said.

"No, you won't," he said. "One box per customer."

"Why's that?"

"We're nearly out of ammunition," he said, waving at the shelves as if it should have been obvious to me.

Wondering if there'd been a Christmas run on bullets (this was rural Michigan, after all), I said, "Why's that?"

He snorted as if I were mentally defective. "You noticed that black guy[1] who just got elected?"

"Obama?"

"There's another?" He squinted at me.

"What's he got to do with your ammunition?"

"He's going to take away our goddamn[2] guns and ban ammo. People are stocking up! Where the hell[3] have you been?"

"I didn't know Obama wanted to take away my guns," I said tentatively.

He snorted again and then pulled a cellphone from his back pocket, poked the screen, and scrolled down for a moment. "Look," he said, holding the phone in front of me where I could read it. It was an email titled, in bold screaming type, "Obama is coming for your guns in January!"

"How do you know?" I said.

"Can't you effing read?"

"Yeah, but that doesn't make it true. There's lots of crap on the internet."

He shook his head. "It's true, I seen it on Fox, too. And you can only buy one box."

I sighed and handed him my driver's license and credit card. You can't challenge Fox News in this part of the country.

The great ammunition shortage of December 2008 was the first of two—the second, coincidentally, was in December 2012, right after President Obama was reelected. An explosion of hysterical emails and widespread coverage of Obama's "coming gun extermination program" preceded both. Which is pretty ironic, given that the only gun effort Obama had undertaken was to allow them in national parks. Nonetheless, these were such large, nationwide events that there's even a Wikipedia page about it all.[4]

Between the weapons manufacturers and right-wing pundits trying to whip up fear and increase donations and listenership, a black man in the White House was a huge boon for the death industry. Earlier in the year, as Barack Obama and Joe Biden were gaining on John McCain and Sarah Palin, Nancy Lanza got a divorce from her husband and, with her son Adam (who was to become the Newtown, Connecticut, shooter), began collecting guns.[5]

It was a fateful year.

While the United States has a long and sordid history of violence against both indigenous people and enslaved people, it's largely in the past 40 years that we've seen an explosion in something virtually unknown in the rest of the world: school shootings.

Tracking that outburst of school-based violence, the past 40 years have also seen an actual *decrease* in all crime, violent crime, and gun-related violence. The three most likely factors causing this decrease are the aging of the baby boomer generation (people in their 20s and 30s are the most likely to engage in criminal activity); the legalization of abortion in 1973, leading to fewer unwanted children (unwanted children are more likely to grow up antisocial); and the removal of lead from gasoline in the 1970s (lead damages the brains of children in ways demonstrated to make them more likely to grow up violent).[6]

That said, with our nation awash in guns, the rate of gun violence on a per capita basis in the United States, at 120 killings per 100,000 people, is massively higher than in any other fully developed nation in the world.[7] In Japan, the odds of a person being killed by a gun are the same as those of being hit by lightning: one in 10 million. In England and Poland, it's one in a million; and in countries with widespread (although reasonable) levels of gun ownership, like Germany, Austria, and the Netherlands, it's one in two million.

In the United States, there are 96 gun-based deaths a day, every day of the year.[8]

This book examines the sources of this proclivity for gun violence that's so deeply embedded in the American psyche. By learning and understanding our history, we can begin the process of recovering from it. Finally, you'll find clear, simple, and effective solutions (that work within the boundaries of the Constitution as interpreted by the Supreme Court) to our gun-violence crisis.

The Social Cost of Guns

In my lifetime, we have lost a President, a Civil Rights leader and a Presidential candidate—all to gun violence.

–Marianne Williamson[1]

It was the late 1960s, and Clark Stinson had joined the army. It wasn't that he wanted to go fight in Vietnam; he hoped that by joining up, he could get a job that would allow him to avoid combat duty. And he'd probably get drafted if he didn't join, given his lottery number.

He came home to Lansing, Michigan, from boot camp on a brief leave extremely depressed. A year before, Clark had joined his best friend—they were inseparable through several years of middle school—spending a summer living in a tee-pee in Michigan's Upper Peninsula, where they both studied religion and meditation practice deep inside the Cherokee National Forest.

When he looked up his friend, he noted that it was Christmastime, and the Vietnam War was still raging. He wanted out of the army but knew that pretty much every option available to him would lead either to exile or to jail. His friend listened attentively but couldn't offer anything other than sympathy.

Two days later, Clark made a decision. He visited a gun store near his home and bought a small pistol and a box of bullets. He went home, sat on his bed, and thought about his future for an hour or so. Then he put the gun in his mouth and pulled the trigger.

His wife, Colleen, called me in hysterics. I was Clark's best friend, the guy he'd confided his depression to, although he never told me that he was considering suicide. It was a shattering experience for all of us who knew and loved Clark.

Society lost an extraordinary human being. I lost my best friend, and Clark's mother lost her son. Colleen lost her husband.

Every year in America, the firearms industry sells about 16 million new weapons into the American civilian mainstream (generating more than enough profits to fund pro-gun groups and PR), while this nation suffers around 34,000 gun-related deaths.[2] Two-thirds of all American gun deaths are suicides, the result of the efficiency of guns at producing a quick and painless death (although they leave a gruesome mess for survivors), combined with continuous access in gun-owning households so that a momentary depressive impulse that could be backed away from via a second thought with an overdose or a slit wrist becomes, instead, nearly 100 percent fatal.

The role of impulse combined with availability becomes starkly visible when compared with the experiences of other countries. For example, when Australia put into place stringent gun-control measures and a nationwide gun-buyback program in 1996, the already-declining annual rate of *all* suicidal deaths, which had fallen by roughly 3 percent, fell dramatically to a more than 7 percent annual decline.[3]

Additionally, the percentage of all homicides committed with guns—74.5 percent in 2016 in the United States[4]—also went down in Australia with the 45 percent drop in gun ownership that immediately followed the introduction of more stringent gun laws.[5] That drop was similar to the drop in suicides. The peer-reviewed journal *Injury Prevention* noted, "Australia's 1996 gun law reforms were followed by more than a decade free of fatal mass shootings, and accelerated declines in firearm deaths, particularly suicides. Total homicide rates followed the same pattern."[6]

The social cost of gun homicides and suicides in the United States—including lost productivity, the "value" of the lost lives, and expenses directly associated with gun deaths—is, according to peer-reviewed research performed by Timothy M. Smith of the University of Minnesota, around $300 billion annually, more than the entire nation was spending on Medicaid in 2013 when the research was published.[7] That works out, essentially, to a $2,380 annual tax on every American household.[8]

And that number doesn't include the more than 80,000 firearms-related injuries reported to the Centers for Disease Control and Prevention (CDC) every year, each costing more than twice as much as other injury-related hospitalizations, because bullets cause such extensive damage to organs, bones, and tissue.[9]

It's hard to know exactly how many children are killed or maimed by guns because in 1996, Rep. Jay Dickey, R-Ark., at the behest of the National Rifle Association (NRA) and weapons manufacturers, attached the Dickey Amendment to a must-pass omnibus spending bill, making it illegal for the CDC to keep track of or analyze the data. Congress simultaneously cut the CDC's budget by the exact amount it had been spending to track gun violence.[10] (Sixteen years later, Dickey essentially apologized in a *Washington Post* op-ed, calling for research into gun violence.[11] As he later told ABC, "I wish I had not been so reactionary."[12])

A peer-reviewed study published in *Pediatrics* in 2017 attempted to determine how many children are the victims of guns in the United States every year and concluded, "Nearly 1300 children die and 5790 are treated for gunshot wounds each year."[13] That's around 19 children shot in this country every day, seven days a week, including holidays.[14]

But that's the bottom of the range of numbers, because above what can be clearly identified, the data gets fuzzy (due to the Dickey Amendment, which is still law).

A 2013 study of New York childhood gun fatalities found that the state suffers from the same problem as other states: a lack of good data. The authors report, "[A] New York Times review of hundreds of child firearm deaths found that accidental shootings occurred roughly twice as often as the records indicate, because of idiosyncrasies in how such deaths are classified by the authorities."[15]

And all of this deals with these deaths and injuries as if they were a purely economic problem, measurable in dollars and cents. But for any family who lost a member of their household to a bullet, whether by suicide or homicide, or even has to deal with the often life-changing consequences of a bullet ripping apart a relative's body but not killing him or her, it becomes obvious that these emotional costs, which can echo through generations, are even more massive.

The social and human costs of a nation awash in firearms are increasingly obvious. Because it is impossible to understand the present without understanding the past, this book covers the history of genocide and slavery, which forms the bedrock of United States history, and how the Second Amendment was ratified to preserve that racist bedrock.

The second part of this book examines the myths at the root of modern American gun culture, and how modern gun culture hatched out of reactions to social and economic changes in the United States, as well as savvy marketing, legal maneuvering, and marketing by weapons manufacturers.

The final chapters of this book analyze the present situation and lay out an array of solutions to "cure" America of its gun-violence epidemic.

CHAPTER 1

The Unholy Alliance of Racism, Genocide, and Guns

*If I had my life to live over, I would die fighting rather
than be a slave again. I want no man's yoke
on my shoulders no more.*

–Robert Falls, age 97, Knoxville, Tennessee[1]

In Isaiah 14:21, the Lord tells Isaiah, "Prepare for his sons a place of slaughter because of the iniquity of their fathers." It's a variation on the old story of karma and seems in a very real way to be playing out today in the United States.

America is facing an epidemic—public health officials use that word—of gun-related suicides, accidents, and even homicides and police killings. That epidemic has grown worse in the past decade, largely because the number of guns in America has increased—in large part because of the racial fears of white men who bought guns in record numbers for eight years during the time in office of America's first black president.

A landmark 1999 study from researchers Franklin Zimring and Gordon Hawkins showed that the main correlation —far surpassing mental illness, socioeconomic status, or race—that could be defined as causal in predicting the rates of gun deaths is a simple number: the number of guns distributed among society.

In the 30 years since that study, Zimring and Hawkins's results have been replicated and re-analyzed dozens of times.[2]

As the American Academy of Pediatrics said in a release published in AAAS's *Science* magazine, "New research shows dramatic differences in the number of children hospitalized and killed each year in the U.S. from firearm-related injuries based on their states' gun legislation, even after adjusting for poverty, unemployment, and education rates. It found twice as many pediatric firearm deaths in states with the most lenient gun regulations compared with states where gun laws are strictest."

They added that this is a critical issue for children, quoting Stephanie Chao, MD, the lead author of the abstract. "Firearm-related injuries are the second leading cause of death among children in the United States," she wrote, "but we found a clear discrepancy in where those deaths happen that corresponds with the strength of states' firearm legislation. In states with lenient laws, children die at alarmingly greater rates."[3]

And, unsurprisingly, America not only has unusually lenient gun laws but also has more guns in civilian hands than any other country in the world. America has a bit more than 4 percent of the world's population but holds almost 50 percent of all the guns in civilian hands worldwide—more than 390 million guns. And the more guns a society has, the more gun deaths it will experience.[4]

The NRA and their army of lobbyists have been quite successful in making this happen. During Obama's presidency,
there was a steady and hysterical drumbeat of articles, emails,
and political proclamations by "pro-gun" politicians and think
tanks suggesting that Obama was preparing to take away
everybody's guns at any minute.

There was even a subtext embraced by the hard right that
he wasn't going to stop there; after disarming white Americans, these folks said, Obama was going to intern them in
otherwise-unused "FEMA camps." Flipped-out gun owners
were repeatedly arrested during the Obama years trying to
break into retired or temporarily vacant military facilities and
toxic waste sites, looking for evidence to prove that Obama
was, in fact, preparing the modern-day version of the World
War II–era Japanese internment camps.

White supremacy was the founding notion of this nation.
White Europeans thought themselves so superior to the
human beings they met here in 1492 that Columbus himself
became the first major North American slaver, shipping Taino
"Indians" back to Spain as slaves for the royal family.

"A slave is as good as gold," Columbus wrote to the king
and queen.

Europeans in the Americas then stepped up that game
into a hemisphere-wide campaign of racial genocide, pulling
off the largest multigenerational mass murder in the history of
the world. In the midst of that effort, they also created the legal
mechanisms necessary to define and legally regulate slavery,
and even built those systems into America's founding docu-
ment, the Constitution.

America was birthed in slavery and genocide. And both needed guns.

It was the superior weaponry of guns that gave the European settlers a massive advantage over the bow-and-arrow-equipped Native Americans, and it was the raw power of widespread white ownership of guns in the South that propped up the institution of slavery for hundreds of years. Without guns, neither would have been possible, or at least neither would have been as easy as they were to pull off.

And now, after centuries of guns being used to kill off and keep down people of color in America, those same guns are creating a terrifying epidemic of gun-facilitated violence from public schools to private homes and public concerts.

It's enough to make one think that Isaiah was on to something.

CHAPTER 2

The Sanitized History of America

Political language is designed to make lies sound truthful and murder respectable, and to give an appearance of solidity to pure wind.

–George Orwell, *Politics and the English Language*

The United States' expansion and conquest in the late 18th century, through the 19th century, and into the 20th century is a history written by white men, inked in the blood of Native Americans, and built on the broken and bloodied backs of enslaved people brought here from Africa.

From 1791, when the Bill of Rights went into effect, until the end of the Civil War, the Second Amendment protected the rights only of white men to own guns. This is simply because until the ratification of the 14th Amendment, states determined who was recognized as a "person" protected under the Constitution.

Initially, in most states, this meant that white men who owned land and paid taxes were the only people considered full citizens under the Constitution.

In the South, white men with guns formed slave patrols to control slaves and formed posses to hunt escaped slaves.

Individuals on the frontier organized to "protect" recently stolen land and to ensure that Native Americans continued to march westward at the point of a gun.

The early 19th century brought us the original Texas Rangers, who were well-armed, and though Hollywood now tells stories about the Texas Rangers as noble lawmen serving on a dangerous frontier, Roxane Dunbar-Ortiz describes a different reality in her book *Loaded*: "Like slave patrols in the Deep South, the Texas Rangers—formed primarily to kill Comanches, eliminate native communities, and control colonized Mexicans to take their land—also hunted down enslaved Africans escaping to freedom. They began to operate in the 1820s, even before . . . Texas had seceded from Mexico in 1836, when Mexico formally outlawed slavery."[1]

What many schoolchildren learn about this period is sanitized. Worse yet, what many adults think they know about this period is not only sanitized but steeped in pop cultural references that glamorize the period while glossing over the utter brutality of American history.

Americans learn about the expansion of America, about the Louisiana Purchase, and about manifest destiny. The images of this period are of elite sharpshooters on the frontier: Daniel Boone, Davy Crockett, and James "Jim" Bowie, to name a few.

And as when there is a mass shooting today, most Americans remember the man who shouldered the rifle more than the person who stared down the barrel. Americans, particularly white Americans, simply ignore the most brutal aspects of the massive slave economy that this country was built on.

American culture and education have hidden the brutality of American history and slavery so effectively that Nevada rancher Cliven Bundy wondered in 2014 whether black Americans were "better off as slaves."[2] More recently, former Alabama Senate candidate Roy Moore told an audience that "[America] was great at the time when families were united—even though we had slavery—they cared for one another."[3]

Likewise, when contemplating the Louisiana Purchase, history talks of Napoleon selling French territory to Thomas Jefferson. The truth is that the Native American population dramatically outnumbered the French population in the Louisiana Territory at that time.

As well-armed Americans poured across the newly purchased territory, Native Americans had three options: continue to flee westward; submit to American conquest and assimilate; or fight back against the rifle-toting American frontiersmen, which would only give more justification for Americans to respond with more force.

Even during this period of slavery and genocide, white Americans didn't necessarily see themselves as murderers and plunderers. The 19th century in America was a period of intense religious revival. On the one hand, the abolition movement rooted itself in Christianity. On the other hand, slave owners pointed to Bible verses showing that slavery had been legitimized in the Old Testament and that black people were heathens who had fallen from God's grace, so slave owners were in fact helping their slaves along the road to salvation.

Native Americans were similarly called heathens and beasts, justifying the murder of those who wouldn't convert and then the taking of their land. It was, after all, God's will and manifest destiny that Americans continue to settle westward. Thus, the American frontiersman set out with his rifle, seeking his God-promised homestead and willing to kill any heathen that stood in his way.

For much of American history, most guns were owned by slaveholders and frontiersmen; urban Americans had little use for guns.

Guns were tools used to hunt animals for food, to keep slaves in line, and to force Native Americans to submit to American conquest, not symbols of manhood or cultural identity. The gun-manufacturing industry wasn't yet selling guns on the mythology of the Minuteman.

But through the 19th century, private gun ownership still wasn't particularly common. Historian Michael Bellesiles told the *Economist* in 1999, "It would appear that at no time prior to 1850 did more than a tenth of the people own guns."[4]

In the years following the Civil War, though, private gun ownership exploded. The explosion of guns in private hands was in part because of the rise of private rifle clubs and paramilitary groups like the Ku Klux Klan, and in part because of savvy marketing by Oliver Winchester, founder of the Winchester Repeating Arms Company.

To understand the roots of the Second Amendment and the roots of American gun culture today, it's vital to examine America's brutal history of gun violence.

It is comfortable to tell a history of America that glamorizes the Old South by ignoring the brutality of slavery. It is easy to turn the frontiersman into a folk hero by breezing over the racism and guerrilla violence that marked the frontlines of America's expansion westward.

But such comfortable histories of America do a disservice and prevent a true understanding of the cultural depths of America's gun-violence epidemic, which, in turn, prevents a clear-eyed assessment of ways to address the problem at its roots.

CHAPTER 3

The Roots of American Gun Culture in the "Discovery" of America

The immediate objects are the total destruction and devastation of their settlements and the capture of as many prisoners of every age and sex as possible. It will be essential to ruin their crops now in the ground and prevent their planting more.

–Orders of George Washington to Major General John Sullivan, May 31, 1779[1]

Without America's history of slavery and Native American genocide, today's "American gun culture" wouldn't exist. The fact that America is today soaked in gun-splattered blood should be no surprise; this nation's story is one of the most genocidal in the modern history of the world.

How bad was it?

In 1992, historian David Stannard set out to determine how many Native Americans were killed, both directly at the barrel of a gun and indirectly by disease and loss of land/food, by European invaders to the Americas.[2] His best estimate puts Hitler to shame: white people killed more than 100 million Native Americans between 1492 and today . . . and the killing continues, in subtler ways than previous generations could have imagined.

One gray, rainy winter day in 2016, Louise and I made our way through the Smithsonian's National Museum of the American Indian. The gift shop sells a map of North America, circa 1491—the year before Columbus blundered onto our shores. On the map, in meticulous detail, are identified the names and lands of the hundreds of native tribes that filled our continent.

There was virtually no empty space at all, except in places like the desert Southwest, but even in the most uninhabitable places there were still people, albeit with population densities as low as a few dozen people per square mile.

Haiti is a great (or terrible) example of what happened when Europeans invaded the Americas and kicked off an orgy of killing of natives, in this case in the Caribbean, by white invaders—a blood frenzy that lasted several centuries, as I described in my book *The Last Hours of Ancient Sunlight*.[3]

When Columbus first landed on Hispaniola (the Caribbean island comprising modern-day Haiti and the Dominican Republic) in 1492, almost the entire island was covered by lush forest. The Taino "Indians" who lived there had an idyllic life prior to Columbus, according to the reports left to us by literate members of Columbus's crew, such as Miguel Cuneo.

It's unclear exactly how well armed Columbus and his crew were when they set out to find a sea route to India. In a 2013 NPR article titled "The First Gun in America," reporter Linton Weeks spoke with Jim Supica, director of the NRA National Firearms Museum in Virginia. Supica told Weeks that for tax purposes, Spanish explorations only listed the *cannons* aboard a vessel, not personal firearms.[4]

In the same NPR article, underwater archaeologist Donald Keith explained that Columbus's crew had a designated "artilleryman," and in at least one instance, Columbus fired his cannons to strike fear into the hearts of the Taino.

Keith told NPR that "when [Columbus] sailed away from Haiti he ordered a shot to be fired through the shipwrecked hulk of the *Santa Maria* to impress on the Native Americans the power of European firearms. The weapon he used would have been a breech-loading wrought-iron cannon. If he had such a weapon he would also have had smaller shoulder arms, such as arquebuses."

Christopher Columbus was armed not only to find gold, but also to dominate and enslave anyone who stood between him and his pursuit of riches.

CHAPTER 4

From Columbus to Jamestown

They have neither the intelligence, the industry, the moral habits, nor the desire of improvement which are essential to any favorable change in their condition. Established in the midst of another and a superior race, and without appreciating the causes of their inferiority or seeking to control them, they must necessarily yield to the force of circumstances and ere long disappear.
–President Andrew Jackson, in his fifth State of the Union address to Congress, December 3, 1833

When Columbus and his crew arrived on their second visit to Hispaniola, they came with enough cannons, guns, and swords to take captive about 1,600 local villagers who had come out to greet them.

Miguel Cuneo wrote, "When our ships . . . were to leave for Spain, we gathered . . . one thousand six hundred male and female persons of those Indians, and of these we embarked in our ships on February 17, 1495. . . . For those who remained, we let it be known [to the Spaniards who manned the island's fort] in the vicinity that anyone who wanted to take some of them could do so, to the amount desired, which was done."[1]

Cuneo further recalled that he took a beautiful teenage Carib girl as his personal slave, a gift from Columbus himself, but when he attempted to have sex with her, she "resisted with all her strength." So, in his own words, he "thrashed her merci-lessly and raped her."

As a reward, Columbus frequently presented his men with local women to rape. As he exported enslaved Taino to other parts of the world, the sex-slave trade became an important part of his business.

Columbus wrote to a friend in 1500: "A hundred castel-lanoes [a Spanish coin] are as easily obtained for a woman as for a farm, and it is very general and there are plenty of dealers who go about looking for girls; those from nine to ten [years old] are now in demand."

And he wrote to the Spanish monarchs in 1493: "It is pos-sible, with the name of the Holy Trinity, to sell all the slaves which it is possible to sell. . . . Here there are so many of these slaves, and also brazilwood, that although they are living things they are as good as gold."[2]

In this regard, the Spaniards carried a thought-virus or world view that's very much alive today in America: the notion that nonwhite peoples are inferior and not fully human, and thus appropriately bought, sold, and controlled with violence and guns.

However, the Taino turned out not to be particularly good workers on the plantations that the Spaniards (and later the French) established on Hispaniola: they resented the Europe-ans who stole the lands and their children, and they attempted to fight back against the invaders or they fled.

Since the Taino were obviously standing in the way of Spain's progress, Columbus sought to impose discipline on them.

Columbus referred to the Taino Indians as cannibals, but there has never been any evidence that this was so. It was apparently a story made up by Columbus—which is to this day still taught in some US schools—to help justify his slaughter and enslavement of the people.

Throughout history, when a culture wages a campaign of brutality and genocide, it's typically invented stories of the enemy's brutality and inhumanity to justify the culture's own brutality.

Columbus's men would cut off an Indian's nose or ear for even a minor offense, so that the Indian could go back to his village to impress the people with Spanish brutality. Columbus and his men attacked the Taino with dogs, skewered them on poles from anus to mouth, and shot them.

Eventually, life for the Taino became so unbearable that, as Pedro de Córdoba wrote to King Ferdinand in a 1517 letter:

> As a result of the sufferings and hard labor they
> endured, the Indians choose and have chosen suicide.
> Occasionally a hundred have committed mass suicide.
> The women, exhausted by labor, have shunned concep-
> tion and childbirth.... Many, when pregnant, have
> taken something to abort and have aborted. Others after
> delivery have killed their children with their own hands,
> so as not to leave them in such oppressive slavery.[3]

Eventually, Columbus, and later his brother Bartholomew Columbus, whom he left in charge of the island, simply resorted to wiping out the Taino altogether.

A similar pattern played out on continental North America over the course of the next two centuries: English settlers first attempted to dominate the Native American tribes that populated the continent and then eventually changed tactics from enslavement to genocide. And genocide was made more efficient with every improvement of European gun technology.

Prior to Columbus's arrival, most scholars place the population of Haiti/Hispaniola at around 300,000 people. By 1496, it was down to 110,000, according to a census done by Bartholomew Columbus. By 1516, the indigenous population was 12,000, and, according to the most famous of Columbus's missionaries, the priest Bartolomé de Las Casas (who was there), by 1542 fewer than 200 natives were alive. The census of 1555 found every single one dead.

From Columbus in Haiti to Cortez in Mexico to John Smith in Virginia, European settlers used their firearms to dominate or wipe out the indigenous people. They were able to do so not because the Spanish or English soldiers outnumbered the Taino in Haiti, the Aztecs in Mexico, or the Powhatan in Virginia, but simply because they possessed more destructive and more lethal weaponry: guns.

From Genocide to Slavery

The settler and pioneer at bottom had justice on their side; this great continent could not have been kept as nothing but a game preserve for squalid savages. Moreover, to the most oppressed Indian nations the whites often acted as a protection, or, at least, they deferred instead of hastening their fate.

–Theodore Roosevelt, *The Winning of the West, Vol. 1*, 1889

The bloody and violent dimensions of today's uniquely American gun culture have deep roots in the genocide of Native Americans.

Author and professor of American studies David E. Stannard writes eloquently about that blood-drenched era in his 1992 book *American Holocaust*, noting that the "vast majority" of native peoples in North America had been exterminated "within no more than a handful of generations following their first encounters with Europeans."[1]

Stannard writes that the "depopulation" rate in most historical and contemporaneous sources is between 90 and 98 percent, so that "for every twenty natives alive at the moment of European contact—when the lands of the Americas teemed with tens of millions of people—only one stood in their place when the bloodbath was over." He adds, "The destruction of the Indians of the Americas was, far and away, the most massive act of genocide in the history of the world."

Racism, racial pseudoscience, and greed ignited a hellfire of death and destruction that stretched, in the Americas, from the Arctic Circle in the north to the Strait of Magellan in the south. Europeans were told by their kings and priests that the people they were exterminating were merely heathens. To the extent that they were human, death would liberate them to heaven.

Scientists of the day proclaimed that Indians weren't even fully human, the same as they had declared of Africans. Thus Indians were suitable for the slave trade or for extermination.

That the European invaders had internalized this narrative is summed up well in an anecdote from a book written by Diego de Landa, a Franciscan monk who was sent in 1554 to the Yucatán to convert the natives to Christianity. In 1566, upon his return to Spain, he published a book titled *Relación de las Cosas de Yucatán* ("A List of Things in the Yucatán"). Both David E. Stannard and the Bulgarian-French historian and author of *Memory as a Remedy for Evil,* Tzvetan Todorov,[2] refer to de Landa's story of Europeans meeting a three-year-old Indian boy:

> *There was one little child, probably three years old, just big enough to walk through the sand. The Indians had gone ahead, and this little child was behind following after them. The little fellow was perfectly naked, travelling on the sand.*
>
> *I saw one man get off his horse, at a distance of about seventy-five yards, and draw up his rifle and fire—he missed the child. Another man came up and said, "Let me try the son of a bitch; I can hit him." He got down off*

his horse, kneeled down and fired at the little child, but
he missed him.

A third man came up and made a similar remark,
and fired, and the little fellow dropped.[3]

This story is remarkable not only for the callous brutality wrought by Spaniards in the Yucatán but also for its demonstration of how limited gun technology has historically been, from the time of Europeans' first arrivals until the early 20th century. Today, a single gunman can use an AR-15 to gun down a roomful of children in nearly the same amount of time as it took three men to fire three shots at a single child in the 16th century—and this was the case well into the 19th century.

The history of commissioned killers telling stories to dehumanize their targets is as old, no doubt, as humanity. And it still works today: witness the anti-Semitism and racism of the modern white supremacy movement that has taken hold of much of the Republican Party (as, with Nixon's "southern strategy," they explicitly picked up the bigots who used to populate the southern Democratic Party); the slaughters taking place in the Middle East and Myanmar; and the way Hitler turned an entire continent into a killing machine against Jews, gypsies, and other *"untermenschen"* ("subhumans").

The Spanish conquerors thought so little of the Mayans that they destroyed and discarded their culture, de Landa recorded: "These people also used special characters or letters with which they recorded in their books their histories and knowledge, as well as figures, and particular signs in those figures explained it all, and lent it meaning and understanding.

We found a great number of books containing such letters, and as they did not contain an iota in which there was not superstition and falsehoods of the devil, we burned them all, which dismayed and distressed them greatly."[4]

So here, then, are several influences on modern American gun culture. There was the need to use guns to perpetrate a massive, continent-wide genocide; there was the need to develop individual gun skills to take on the Indian woodsmen who'd been targeted for genocide; and there was the need to keep slaves from revolting while terrorizing them into working and reproducing.

Howard Zinn notes in *The People's History of the United States* that in colonial Virginia, a law was passed as early as 1639 decreeing that "all persons except Negroes" were to get arms and ammunition.[5]

Zinn speculates that the arms were likely used to fight Virginia's Indian population. The law, however, doubly empowered the European settlers, who wielded their guns both to eradicate the Indians and to subjugate the colony's growing number of black slaves. Virginia was only one of several American colonies with such a law on the books.

To commit the largest genocide in known human history, a society must create an implacable police state to terrorize millions of people into remaining in slavery. And to maintain that police structure to prevent those former slaves and genocide victims from fully participating in modern society, the society will need guns. Lots of guns.

Early Hints toward the Second Amendment

The only good Indians I ever saw were dead.
–General Philip Henry Sheridan, 1869

The winter of 1610 in Jamestown, Virginia, is simply known as the "starving time." Many settlers fled to join the Powhatan Indians to keep from starving. When summer arrived, the colonial governor sent a message to the Indians asking for the English settlers to be returned.

It's unclear exactly how the Powhatan tribe responded, but the colony reported to the English that they received "noe other than prowde and disdaynefull answers."[1]

The Powhatan people most likely fed the refugee settlers and gave them shelter and hospitality, but the Virginia governor nonetheless dispatched soldiers to get "revenge."

Howard Zinn, in his *People's History of the United States*, reports that when the soldiers found an Indian encampment, their actions demonstrated that the English could be every bit as brutal as Columbus was in Haiti.

Zinn writes that the soldiers "killed fifteen or sixteen Indians, burned the houses, cut down the corn growing around the village, took the queen of the tribe and her children into boats, then ended up throwing the children overboard 'and shoteinge owtt their Braynes in the water'" ("shooting out their brains in the water").

These types of gun-based skirmishes became common on what was then the American frontier—and 12 years later, Zinn reports, "the Indians, alarmed as the English settlements kept growing in numbers, apparently decided to try to wipe them out for good. They went on a rampage and, lacking guns, nonetheless massacred 347 men, women, and children with knives, bows and arrows, and spears. From then on it was total war."[2]

Thus, genocidal battles on the frontier helped to lay the groundwork for America's gun culture. Howard Zinn calls it "total war," while other historians, such as Roxane Dunbar-Ortiz and John Grenier, referred to these conflicts as "savage war."

These historians draw a direct line from colonial "savage war" to the Second Amendment, and to modern US warfare and the militarization of American police via the war on drugs.

"Today, called 'special operations' or 'low-intensity conflict,'" Dunbar-Ortiz writes, "that kind of warfare was first used against Indigenous communities by colonial militias. . . . These voluntary fighting crews made up of individual civilians—'rangers'—are the groups referenced as *militias*, as they came to be called, in the Second Amendment."[3]

Here, again, is part of the Second Amendment's roots—in genocide and in the centuries-long "total war" that European settlers waged against Native Americans.

CHAPTER 7

Gun Culture's Ebb and Flow

> *[Using guns,] Pizarro captured Atahuallpa within a few minutes after the two leaders first set eyes on each other. Pizarro proceeded to hold his prisoner for eight months, while extracting history's largest ransom in return for a promise to free him. After the ransom—enough gold to fill a room 22 feet long by 17 feet wide to a height of over 8 feet—was delivered, Pizarro reneged on his promise and executed Atahuallpa.*
>
> **–Jared Diamond, *Guns, Germs, and Steel***

"Not until the New Englanders learned to fight like Indians could they defeat the Indians," writes David Kopel in a *Washington Post* article titled, "The American Indian foundation of gun culture."[1]

Kopel shows that the British had been so afraid, for so many centuries, of peasant uprisings that they banned guns and didn't encourage military marksmanship. Thus, there was virtually no "gun culture" in 17th-century England, so the whole idea of sharpshooters (like King Arthur's bowmen of Middle Ages England) had died out.

The result was that when British soldiers in North America went off to kill Indians, they did so arrayed in straight lines and with brute-force shooting—whichever side fired the most bullets generally killed the most guys on the other side.

But the Indians of North America didn't cooperate like European armies and just stand in a conspicuous line to be shot at.

They grew up in a hunting and gathering culture, by and large, that emphasized skill and stealth. They hid behind trees and hills, sneaked up behind British forces, and even set traps for the hapless Brits.

On the American frontier, that meant that even with superior firepower, the English were routinely suffering losses to the Indians. The Indians knew the land better, and they were fighting to protect a homeland that had sustained the Indians and their culture for thousands of years.

In his history of early Virginia, titled *American Slavery, American Freedom*, Edmund S. Morgan writes that in the middle of the 17th century, "[s]ince the Indians were better woodsmen than the English and virtually impossible to track down, the method was to feign peaceful intentions, let them settle down and plant their corn wherever they chose, and then, just before harvest, fall upon them, killing as many as possible and burning the corn."[2]

Without trickery and guns, early American settlers would have been wiped out by Native Americans on their own land. But guns (and a fondness for violent brutality) made the difference.

As Thomas Jefferson wrote on August 2, 1816, reflecting on that era to his protégé James Madison, "After Braddock's defeat, on the Monongahela in 1755, the incursions of the Indians on our frontiers spread panic and dismay thro' the whole country; insomuch that it was scarcely possible to procure men, either as regulars or militia, to go against them."[3]

But the English settlers were determined to dominate the land they had stolen and settled—and to utterly destroy the indigenous people they encountered on the stolen land.

And that required guns and the marksmanship skills that come with a developing gun culture.

In less than a generation, the European invaders of North America figured out that if they were going to be effective at stealing Indians' land, they'd better quickly become good shots.

Thus, by the time of the American Revolution, George Washington's army—and white people across the continent generally—had become proficient marksmen, and personal gun ownership had become much more commonplace among both "pioneers" and urban wealthy people (guns were as expensive then, relative to income, as cars are now, but nobody was writing gun loans or leases, so they weren't as common as cars are today).

CHAPTER 8

How Slavery Laid the Foundation of the Second Amendment

I think slavery is the next thing to hell.

**–Harriet Tubman to Benjamin Drew,
St. Catharines, Ontario, Canada, 1855**

Europeans used guns and formed loose militias to wage a genocidal war against the once-thriving Native American population in North America. Militias in the South at first served the same role, but as the American frontier pushed westward, the role of local militias shifted.

By the mid-18th century, rich plantation owners located east of the Appalachian frontier were generally protected by the British military, which enforced the treaties between Native American tribes and the British empire.

As a result, white men in the South soon served in militias for a very different purpose. Rather than keeping Native Americans out of the plantations, the militias were deployed to keep African slaves on the plantations—or to return any who may have escaped. These militias were known as "slave patrols," and they were well regulated by the slave states.

In Georgia, for example, a generation before the American Revolution, the colonial government passed laws in 1755

31

and 1757 that required all plantation owners or their white male employees to be members of the Georgia militia and those armed militia members to make monthly inspections of the quarters of all slaves in the state. The law defined which counties had which armed militias and even required armed militia members to keep a keen eye out for slaves who might be planning uprisings.

As Carl T. Bogus wrote for the University of California, Davis, Law Review in 1998, "The Georgia statutes required patrols, under the direction of commissioned militia officers, to examine every plantation each month and authorized them to search 'all Negro Houses for offensive Weapons and Ammunition' and to apprehend and give twenty lashes to any slave found outside plantation grounds."[1]

It's the answer to the question posed by the character played by Leonardo DiCaprio in *Django Unchained* when he asks, "Why don't they just rise up and kill the whites?" If the movie were real, it would have been a purely rhetorical question, because every southerner of the era knew the simple answer: well-regulated militias kept the slaves in chains.

Sally E. Hadden, in her book *Slave Patrols: Law and Violence in Virginia and the Carolinas*, writes, "Although eligibility for the militia seemed all-encompassing, not every middle-aged white male Virginian or Carolinian became a slave patroller." There were exemptions so that "men in critical professions," like judges, legislators, and students, could stay at their work.[2]

Generally, though, she documents how most southern men between 18 and 45—including physicians and ministers—had to serve on slave patrol in the militia at one time or another in their lives.

And slave rebellions were keeping the slave patrols busy.

By the time the Constitution was ratified, hundreds of substantial slave uprisings had occurred across the South. Blacks outnumbered whites in large areas, and the state militias were used to both prevent and put down slave uprisings. Slavery can exist only in the context of a police state, and the enforcement of that police state was the explicit job of the gun-toting slave-patrol militias.[3]

Gun Culture Enshrined: The Second Amendment

*To put on the garment of legitimacy is the
first aim of every coup.*

–Barbara W. Tuchman, *A Distant Mirror:
The Calamitous 14th Century*

There's an old saying, paraphrasing Hitler, that "the winners write history." American culture grew out of genocide, slavery, and white supremacy, and guns have been central to this history, although the white "winners" have largely excised this from modern historical narratives. But the founders knew what was up.

When the Bill of Rights was ratified, the Second Amendment institutionalized guns, as well as the militias, into the fabric of this newly formed nation. But this is, in part, an accident of Constitution history.

Like so many other things that are core to America, the Second Amendment originated in the mind of Thomas Jefferson. Ironically, the slave owner who spent much of his life trying to end slavery gave birth—albeit indirectly—to the amendment necessary to bring the southern states into the union, and thus to keep their slaveholding institutions intact.

It started with Jefferson's concern that the new nation he'd helped birth might end up the victim of a military coup because a standing army had risen up during times of peace (as had happened so often in European history). Jefferson disliked and feared standing armies so much that he demanded that James Madison add a ban on them to the Bill of Rights. Otherwise, Jefferson strongly implied (to Madison and many others) that he'd sabotage the Constitution in the Virginia ratifying convention.

Without Virginia's vote for ratification, the Constitution would die.

As a Virginia slave owner, Jefferson knew the importance of the slave-patrol militias that kept down slave uprisings in that state. The governments of Georgia and the Carolinas had already enshrined slave patrols into law. The slave-patrol militias were also well known to the Virginian James Madison, whose slave-powered plantation Montpelier was just a half-day's ride from Jefferson's Monticello.

Neither Jefferson nor Madison thought the Constitution represented a threat to his state's slave patrols. Nonetheless, this issue ultimately forced Madison to make two modifications to the Second Amendment. And those modifications, ironically, ended up leaving standing armies intact—along with the slave-patrol militias in the South.

A Constitutional Rorschach Ploy: Limits on Slavery?

They sold my mother, sister, and brother to old man Askew,
a slave speculator, and they were shipped to the Mississippi
bottoms in a boxcar. I never heard from my mother any more.
I never seed my brother again, but my sister come back to
Charlotte. She come to see me. She married and
lived there till she died.

–Patsy Mitchner, age 84, Raleigh, North Carolina[1]

It was the week before Christmas, 1787. Thomas Jefferson sat at his desk on the ground floor of his rented home, the 22-room townhouse known as the Hôtel de Langeac on the Champs-Elysées, just outside the gates of the city of Paris. Living in the house with him were his daughters, Patsy, 15, and Polly, 9; his personal secretary, William Short; and two of his slaves, 22-year-old James Hemings and 14-year-old Sally Hemings.

The issue of slavery was much discussed in Europe and America at the time. France had declared it illegal, so James and Sally Hemings were both considered free persons when they arrived, and Jefferson paid them each as employees.

Jefferson had just received correspondence from his close friend, fellow plantation owner, and protégé, James Madison. Before him on his desk lay the first draft of a new Constitution for 13 recently liberated states on the North American continent.

For four years since the American Revolution ended, the 13 states had been operating as a loose confederation, functioning pretty much as independent nation-states stitched together with what was largely a trade agreement called the "Articles of Confederation."

Madison's newly proposed Constitution would bring the states into a single union, knit together by a federal government, something functionally lacking under the Articles. It would create the United States of America.

Madison had spent the previous five years studying constitutions ancient and modern, from the Greek and Roman to the Iroquois, and kept the notes throughout the Constitutional Convention that summer in Philadelphia. His knowledge was so deep, his influence so powerful, that to this day he's known as "the father of the Constitution." But he wanted his mentor's thoughts before going further.

Jefferson wrote to Madison from Paris on December 20, 1787, that he would oblige, by "adding a few words on the Constitution proposed by our convention."

"I like much the general idea of framing a government," Jefferson wrote, "which should go on of itself, peaceably, without needing continual recurrence to the State legislatures. I like the organization of the government into legislative, judiciary and executive. I like the power given the legislature to levy taxes, and for that reason solely, I approve of the greater House being chosen by the people directly."

Jefferson was particularly pleased with the House/Senate compromise (small states still got two senators) and the three-fifths and 1808 compromises, which brought together the 13 slave and free states.

Although slavery was arguably protected in the new Constitution, it was only within limits.

For example, the southern states had argued at the Constitutional Convention that because the number of representatives a state got in the House of Representatives was calculated by how many people lived in that state, all of their slaves should be counted in the census every 10 years so that they could have more members representing them (and, thus, more votes and more power) in the House of Representatives. The northern states' representatives pointed out that slaves couldn't vote in the South (freed blacks did vote in several northern states during this era) and therefore should not be counted at all.

The southerners rebutted that there were large numbers of white indentured ("bound to Service") servants in the North (most had indentures to pay off the cost of transporting them from Europe, although some were indentured because of debt or crimes) who also couldn't vote, as well as large numbers of Indians, particularly among the populous six-nation Iroquois Confederacy, who were forbidden to vote. They suggested that if the slaves in the South weren't to be counted toward congressional representation, then those indentured white people and the Indians in the North shouldn't be counted, either.

The compromise worked out was that three-fifths of the slaves in the South would be counted, along with all of the white indentured servants in the North but none of the Indians in any state (except those who'd accepted the white man's life and were working and paying taxes).

They codified it in Article 1, Section 2 of the Constitution, which says: "Representatives and direct Taxes shall be apportioned among the several States which may be included within this Union, according to their respective Numbers, which shall be determined by adding to the whole Number of free Persons, including those bound to Service for a Term of Years, and excluding Indians not taxed, three fifths of all other Persons."

The second limit was that the slave trade into America would end in 1808, although this was a bit of a Rorschach ploy: everybody saw in it what they wanted.

The northern representatives (and some from the South, like Jefferson, although he was not included in the debates) hoped this meant that slavery would fade out of American life quickly after 1808. The majority in the South accepted that date because they figured by then they'd be solidly in the "slave-breeding" business, and cutting off the importation of slaves would raise their value. (At the time of the Constitution's writing, a single slave in good condition had the value of about 100 acres of land.)

That 1808 compromise was put into the Constitution in Article 1, Section 9: "The Migration or Importation of such

Persons as any of the States now existing shall think proper to admit, shall not be prohibited by the Congress prior to the Year one thousand eight hundred and eight . . ."

There were those in the North who objected to the Constitution because it wasn't more explicit about ending slavery. And, similarly, some in the South were openly worried that the Article 1, Section 8, militia powers given to Congress by the Constitution could be used by the North to take away and/or free their slaves by calling them up for military service.

Jefferson wasn't so concerned about the Article 1, Section 8, argument and saw the two compromises as a way to bring the slave and free states together to create the United States.

But it was Jefferson's objection to standing armies during times of peace that led directly to Madison drafting the Second Amendment—and to that amendment being ultimately modified in such a way as to guarantee that the southern states could keep their slave patrols.

CHAPTER 11

How Europe's History of Mercenaries and Military Coups Shaped the Second Amendment

That a well-regulated militia, composed of the body of the people, trained to arms, is the proper, natural and safe defense of a free state; that standing armies, in time of peace, should be avoided as dangerous to liberty; and that, in all cases, the military should be under strict subordination to, and governed by, the civil power.

–George Mason, Virginia Declaration of Rights, June 12, 1776

Thomas Jefferson was one of the many founders who were wary of standing armies during peacetime. The history of Europe, from the then-modern to the ancient, was littered with stories of nations seized or overthrown by their own standing armies in military coups (which continue to this day).

The topic was hotly debated, and Alexander Hamilton wrote an extensive article about it, first published in a newspaper titled the *Daily Advertiser* on January 10, 1788. This article is now known as Volume 29 of *The Federalist Papers*.

"If standing armies are dangerous to liberty," Hamilton wrote, arguing that Article 1, Section 8, took care of the problem, "an efficacious power over the militia, in the body to whose care the protection of the State is committed, ought, as far as possible, to take away the inducement and the pretext to such unfriendly institutions."

A citizens' militia, Hamilton stated, "appears to me the only substitute that can be devised for a standing army, and the best possible security against it." He added, "To render an army unnecessary [by instead having state-based citizens' militias] will be a more certain method of preventing its existence than a thousand prohibitions upon paper."

Jefferson was also morally offended by the idea of a standing army that people would join because they were so poor that there was no other way to get an education and a job (for such people, he wanted universal free public education, including free college tuition, which he brought into being when he founded the tuition-free University of Virginia).

He wrote his thoughts on the topic in a June 18, 1813, letter to his old friend, the future president James Monroe. "It is more a subject of joy that we have so few of the desperate characters which compose modern regular armies," he wrote, pleased that he had radically cut the size of the US army during his tenure as president. "But it proves more forcibly the necessity of obliging every citizen to be a soldier; this was the case with the Greeks and Romans, and must be that of every free State. Where there is no oppression there will be no pauper hirelings."

He noted that so-called voluntary armies depend upon a "pauper class" for their existence.

By the end of his presidency (1808), Jefferson had largely done away with America's standing army, and he was thus inspired to write to his friend Dr. Thomas Cooper, on September 10, 1814, that "our men are so happy at home that they will not hire themselves to be shot at for a shilling a day. Hence we can have no standing armies for defence, because we have no paupers to furnish the materials."

In history, Jefferson found justification for his opinion. "The Greeks and Romans had no standing armies," he wrote in that letter to Monroe, "yet they defended themselves. The Greeks by their laws, and the Romans by the spirit of their people, took care to put into the hands of their rulers no such engine of oppression as a standing army. Their system was to make every man a soldier, and oblige him to repair to the standard of his country whenever that was reared. This made them invincible; and the same remedy will make us so."

He noted that such a system of universal service "was proposed to Congress in 1805, and subsequently; and, on the last trial was lost, I believe, by a single vote only. Had it prevailed, what has now happened [in the War of 1812] would not have happened. Instead of burning our Capitol, we should have possessed theirs in Montreal and Quebec. We must now adopt it, and all will be safe."

He observed that three-quarters of a million men qualified for a draft in 1814 and added, "With this force properly classed, organized, trained, armed and subject to tours of a year of military duty, we have no more to fear for the defence of our country than those who have the resources of despotism and pauperism."

Thus, Jefferson wrote to Madison in that letter from Paris as Christmas approached, "I will now add what I do not like [about this first draft of the Constitution you just shared with me]. First the omission of a bill of rights providing clearly and without the aid of sophisms for freedom of religion, freedom of the press, protection against standing armies, restriction against monopolies, the eternal & unremitting force of the habeas corpus laws, and trials by jury in all matters of fact triable by the laws of the land & not by the law of Nations."

While most of those things made their way into the Constitution, Jefferson's objection to corporate monopolies was left out, as was his "protection against standing armies," with the exception of Article I, Section 8, requiring reauthorization of the army every two years. He was quite emphatic about this: two years later, in July 1788, he implicitly threatened to blow up the Constitution via his influence with the Virginia delegation if his concerns weren't met with a Bill of Rights to protect America from a standing army.

"I sincerely rejoice at the acceptance of our new constitution by nine States," he wrote to Madison from Paris on July 31, 1788. "It is a good canvass, on which some strokes only want retouching. What these are, I think are sufficiently manifested by the general voice from north to south, which calls for a bill of rights. It seems pretty generally understood, that this should go to juries, habeas corpus, standing armies, printing, religion and monopolies."

His threat came in the next paragraph: "But if such cannot be found, then it is better to establish trials by jury, the right of habeas corpus, freedom of the press and freedom of religion, in all cases, and to abolish standing armies in time of peace, and monopolies in all cases, than not to do it in any."

He then made a detailed argument for each of his concerns. With regard to standing armies, he wrote to Madison in that same letter, "If no check can be found to keep the number of standing troops within safe bounds, while they are tolerated as far as necessary, [then] abandon them altogether, discipline well the militia, and guard the magazines with them. More than magazine guards will be useless, if few, and dangerous, if many. . . . I hope, therefore, a bill of rights will be formed, to guard the people against the federal government, as they are already guarded against their State governments, in most instances."

While that last quote from Jefferson is used extensively to argue that he was saying that people should have guns to shoot at the government if it became oppressive, Jefferson, in fact, was arguing something quite different. He (and President Eisenhower echoed his thought, warning us explicitly about the "military-industrial complex") believed that standing armies in time of peace represented a threat to *democracy itself* that could be remedied only with a Switzerland-style citizen militia governed and well regulated by the states.

Jefferson's opinion was nothing radical; bans on standing armies were already law in many states at the time Jefferson was writing to Madison from Paris in 1787. It was an opinion widely shared by the founding generation.

The North Carolina Constitution written in 1776 said, "[A]s standing armies, in time of peace are dangerous to liberty, they ought not to be kept up." Similar language was in the Virginia Bill of Rights of 1776 and the Vermont Constitution of 1777 ("as standing armies, in time of peace, are dangerous to liberty, they ought not to be kept up" in both).

As of 1780, Massachusetts's constitution said, "[A]s standing armies, in time of peace are dangerous to liberty, they ought not to be kept up," and New Hampshire wrote similar language into its constitution in 1784: "Standing armies are dangerous to liberty, and ought not to be raised or kept up without the consent of the legislature."

Similarly, the first draft of the Second Amendment said, "That the people have a right to keep and bear arms; that a well regulated Militia composed of the body of the people trained to arms is the proper, natural and safe defense of a free State. *That standing armies in time of peace are dangerous to liberty, and therefore ought to be avoided as far as the circumstances and protection of the community will admit* [emphasis mine]; and that in all cases the military should be under strict subordination to and governed by the civil power."

Ultimately, to decrease the possibility of a standing army growing large enough to harm government or seize power over a free people, the framers put into Article 1, Section 8, of the Constitution a two-year maximum funding provision. It gave Congress the power "[t]o raise and support Armies, but no Appropriation of Money to that Use shall be for a longer Term than two Years."

Nowhere else in the Constitution is the power of Congress to order up and pay for *anything* restricted in time. But the army—literally, the very *existence* of the standing army—had to be carefully constrained, the framers believed, and thus reevaluated by Congress at least every two years.

CHAPTER 12

How Fears of Abolition Shaped the Second Amendment

Give me liberty or give me death.
–Patrick Henry

Article 1, Section 8, of the proposed Constitution had southern slave owners concerned about the future of their economy.

As discussed earlier, slavery can exist only in the context of a police state, and the enforcement of that police state was the explicit job of the militias.

If the antislavery folks in the North could figure out a way to disband those southern militias—or even just to move the militias out of the states—the police state of the South would collapse. And, similarly, if the North were to invite into military service the slaves of the South, then they could be emancipated, which would collapse the institution of slavery—and the southern economic and social systems—altogether.

These two possibilities worried southerners like James Monroe, George Mason (who owned more than 300 slaves), and the southern Christian evangelical Patrick Henry (the largest slaveholder in the state of Virginia).

Their main concern was that Article 1, Section 8, of the newly proposed Constitution—which gave the federal government the power to raise and supervise a militia—could also allow that federal militia to subsume their state militias and change them from slavery-enforcing institutions into something that could even, one day, free the slaves.

This was not an imagined threat. Famously, 12 years earlier, during the lead-up to the Revolutionary War, Lord Dunsmore offered freedom to slaves who could escape the American South and join his forces. "Liberty to Slaves" was stitched onto the pocket flaps of the escapees' jackets. During the war, British General Henry Clinton extended the practice in 1779. And numerous freed slaves served in General Washington's army.

Thus, southern legislators and plantation owners lived not just in fear of their own slaves rebelling, but also in fear that their slaves could be emancipated through military service.

At the ratifying convention in Virginia in 1788, Patrick Henry laid it out:[1] "Let me here call your attention to that part [Article 1, Section 8, of the proposed Constitution] which gives the Congress power to provide for organizing, arming, and disciplining the militia, and for governing such part of them as may be employed in the service of the United States. . . .

"By this, sir, you see that their control over our last and best defence is unlimited. If they neglect or refuse to discipline or arm our militia, they will be useless: the states can do neither . . . this power being exclusively given to Congress. The power of appointing officers over men not disciplined or armed is ridiculous; so that this pretended little remains of power left to the states may, at the pleasure of Congress, be rendered nugatory."

George Mason expressed a similar fear: "The [slave patrol] militia may be here destroyed by that method which has been practised in other parts of the world before; that is, by rendering them useless, by disarming them. Under various pretences, Congress may neglect to provide for arming and disciplining the militia; and the state governments cannot do it, for Congress has an exclusive right to arm them [under this proposed Constitution]."

Henry then bluntly laid it out: "If the country be invaded, a state may go to war, but cannot suppress [slave] insurrections [under this new Constitution]. If there should happen an insurrection of slaves, the country cannot be said to be invaded. They cannot, therefore, suppress it without the interposition of Congress. . . . Congress, and *Congress only* [under this new Constitution], can call forth the militia."

And why was that such a concern for Patrick Henry?

"In this state," he said, "there are two hundred and thirty-six thousand blacks, and there are many in several other states. But there are few or none in the Northern States. . . . May Congress not say, *that every black man must fight*? Did we not see a little of this last war? We were not so hard pushed as to make emancipation general; but acts of Assembly passed that every slave who would go to the army should be free."

Patrick Henry was also convinced that the power over the various state militias given to the federal government in the new Constitution could be used to strip the slave states of their slave-patrol militias. He knew the majority in the North opposed slavery, and he worried that they'd use the

Constitution to free the South's slaves (a process then called "manumission").

The abolitionists would, he was certain, use that power (and, ironically, this is pretty much what Abraham Lincoln ended up doing): "[T]hey will search that paper [the Constitution], and see if they have power of manumission," said Henry. "And have they not, sir? Have they not power to provide for the general defence and welfare? May they not think that these call for the abolition of slavery? May they not pronounce all slaves free, and will they not be warranted by that power?

"This is no ambiguous implication or logical deduction. The paper [proposed Constitution] speaks to the point: they have the power in clear, unequivocal terms, and will clearly and certainly exercise it."

He added, "This is a local matter, and I can see no propriety in subjecting it to Congress."

James Madison, the "Father of the Constitution" and a slaveholder himself, basically called Patrick Henry paranoid. "I was struck with surprise," Madison said, "when I heard him express himself alarmed with respect to the emancipation of slaves. . . . There is no power to warrant it, in that paper [the Constitution]. If there be, I know it not."

But the southern fears wouldn't go away.

Patrick Henry even argued that southerners' "property" (slaves) would be lost under the new Constitution, and the resulting slave uprising would be a disaster for them: "In this situation," Henry said to Madison, "I see a great deal of the property of the people of Virginia in jeopardy, and their peace and tranquility gone."

So Madison, who had (at Jefferson's insistence) already begun to prepare proposed amendments to the Constitution, changed his first draft to one that addressed the militia issue to make sure it was unambiguous that the southern states could maintain their slave patrol militias.

His first draft for what became the Second Amendment had said: "The right of the people to keep and bear arms shall not be infringed; a well armed, and well regulated militia being the best security of a free *country* [emphasis mine]: but no person religiously scrupulous of bearing arms, shall be compelled to render military service in person."

But Henry, Mason, and others wanted southern states to preserve their slave-patrol militias independent of the federal government. So Madison changed the word "country" to the word "state" and redrafted the Second Amendment into today's form:

"A well regulated Militia, being necessary to the security of a free *State* [emphasis mine], the right of the people to keep and bear Arms, shall not be infringed."

Little did Madison, Jefferson, or Henry realize that one day in the future, weapons-manufacturing corporations, newly defined as "persons" by a dysfunctional Supreme Court, would use his slave-patrol militia amendment to protect their "right" to manufacture and sell guns to individuals who would use them to murder schoolchildren.

CHAPTER 13

The Myth of the
Well-Armed Cowboy

*Leave Your Revolvers at Police Headquarters,
and Get a Check.*

–Signs posted throughout Wichita, Kansas, in 1873 and
typical of other Wild West towns of the era[1]

The now-romanticized cowboys of the Old West were, along
with slaves and Native Americans, the earliest victims of
unregulated capitalism in America.

America was first settled in a big way by the British East
India Company's subsidiary the Virginia Company, at Jamestown (named after King James, the largest holder of stock in the
corporation) in 1607. The land/state claimed by the company
was named Virginia, after the Virgin Queen Elizabeth I, who,
in 1600, signed the charter of the world's first modern-style
limited-liability corporation (the East India Company).

By the time of the American Revolution, the influence of
the company and its subsidiaries had extended so far across the
colonies that small businesses were loudly complaining that it
was nearly impossible for small or midsized companies to exist.

In an open act of revolt against the company and the huge
tax cut it got with the Tea Act of 1773, the citizens of Boston
threw over a million dollars' (in today's money) worth of the

company's tea into the harbor. That set in motion the events that led directly to the Declaration of Independence.

But while a loud revolt against a big business monopoly was happening in the northern states, a far quieter one was happening in the South that would have an equally huge impact.

When they first meaningfully settled in the 17th and early 18th centuries, most southern farmers—even with the use of slaves—ran rather small operations, eking whatever they could by way of subsistence out of land stolen from the Indians.

To protect British textile manufacturers, the East India Company had successfully lobbied the British Parliament to pass a law banning the manufacture in the colonies of any sort of "fine clothing." This predictably resulted in a huge export market for cotton to England, where clothing was manufactured for re-import into America, and by the late 1600s and early 1700s, cotton-arable land in the South had become highly valuable and expensive.

Small farmers found themselves being increasingly squeezed—throughout the 1700s and well into the 1800s— by high land prices, and by monopolistic and predatory shippers, exporters, and bankers. Add to that the jurisdictions that taxed land, and there was a strong incentive for successful cotton producers to grow their plantations to the size where they could have economic and political leverage in the increasingly monopolistic marketplace.

Thus, large plantation owners throughout the era routinely expanded their operations. In the 18th and early 19th centuries, it was largely through the murder of native populations, an effort aggressively aided by the young US government (see Andrew Jackson and the Trail of Tears). Later it was through what today are called buyouts and acquisitions, echoing the farming consolidations of the Reagan era—large slaveholding plantation operators gave their small-farm neighbors offers they couldn't refuse and acquired their lands on the cheap.

With a few bucks in their pockets and pushed off their own land, many of these former southern dirt farmers moved west in search of new opportunities. The Civil War further consolidated the power of the large plantation owners and killed off hundreds of thousands of the smaller farm operators (who were conscripted for the war, the wealthy being able to buy their way out of the draft in both North and South).

These factors combined with the invention and widespread distribution of the cotton gin (1830s) and the railroads (which went transcontinental around the end of the Civil War) to make anything but big operations harder and harder to sustain.

After the Civil War, and particularly with the California gold rush and the widespread romanticizing of the cowboy myth by books and serializations in publications like the *Saturday Evening Post* (first published in 1821), there was an explosion of southern young men and poor families who wanted to move west.

Many, indeed most, of the "bandits" (a friendlier term in that era than "criminals") were former Confederate soldiers who either were running from indictments for war crimes or had returned home from the war to find nothing left.

Some of the most famous of the "Old West outlaws" were these former Confederate soldiers, including Missouri "bush-whackers" (hide-and-shoot terrorists principally among the Missouri Confederates) like former slaveholders Jesse and Frank James. The bushwhackers were responsible, for example, for the 1863 slaughter of more than 150 men and boys in Lawrence, Kansas, an antislavery town.

America was birthed in genocide, killing as many as 100 million Native Americans over the course of five centuries, and in the early 1870s the country had just completed a bloody civil war over the enslavement of people brought here from Africa.

Good white citizens, however, weren't much interested in reading that we'd outdone every other country in the history of the world at genocide, or that we'd fought a war to preserve an institution anathema to the high-sounding concepts laid out in the Declaration of Independence.

Out of this came the myth of the cowboy.

While in fact most actual cowboys were hardworking ranch hands and cattle herders, poorly paid and worked to death in often terrible weather, the fictional version sold to America in the post–Civil War era was an entirely different thing. Even the most brutal and sociopathic outlaws, like the James brothers and the James–Younger Gang, were transformed into tragic-but-noble figures by the pens of America's novelists and magazine writers.

Overlooking their roles as criminals, rapists, and murderers was only part of the fictionalization of the Old West. Guns came with it.

In order for a fictional protagonist to be heroic, he must have some sort of super-ability. He must be so extraordinary at *something* that he can be turned into a legend, into someone to emulate—into, well, a *hero*.

And the heroic ability that America's press fell in love with through the late 19th century was gunfighting.

Prior to the Civil War, most guns were handmade and thus quite expensive and often unreliable. The steel of the day was vulnerable to rust unless fastidiously maintained, and soft enough that weapons didn't have a particularly long life if they were frequently fired.

That all changed with Samuel Colt's patent in 1835 on a factory-manufactured rifle. The whole concept was in its infancy at the time, and Colt's weapons had significant quality problems, to the point that by 1842 the US government was loudly complaining about his guns and he closed his factory.

Colt took a second run at it in 1846 to supply guns for the Mexican-American War, going into business first with Eli Whitney (the wealthy inventor of the cotton gin) and later branching into his own company. By the end of the Civil War, Colt weapons were the sparkling new technology of the era, and Colt himself was hailed as a visionary entrepreneur the way Steve Jobs is today.

Eager to jump on the bandwagon of the newest toys for boys, writers turned bushwhackers and common thieves who were competent gunslingers into the stuff of legend.

The shootout at the OK Corral didn't happen at the OK Corral but instead in a narrow alley and was probably just a plain, old-fashioned bushwhack? No problem—simply rewrite the story. Jesse James had been a slave owner and was generally hated by everybody he came into contact with? No problem—simply reinvent him as a noble hero. Daniel Boone was just a pelt trapper and scavenger who couldn't keep a job or a relationship? No problem—make him a legend.

From the *Saturday Evening Post* of the 1870s to Clint Eastwood's Josey Wales, the legends were there to be made.

And layered on top of it all was the idea that there were people—lots of them—who occupied this continent and needed to be killed.

The "Indians" were savage beasts who couldn't be tamed or taught. The Africans brought here to work the fields were just one step up the evolutionary ladder from gorillas—a common theme in the art of the 19th century and before—and therefore didn't fully experience "human" emotions or pain. (This so persists to this day that African-American patients in America's hospitals are *today* less likely to be given painkillers or the same doses of painkillers as white patients.)[2]

Herbert Spencer took Charles Darwin's theory of biological evolution and applied it to society, creating a concept often referred to as social Darwinism, which brought the final part of the formula into the mix. Instead of Jefferson's random diary musings about the equality of the Indians to whites[3] or the inferiority of blacks, here now was an actual theory that took the white world by storm.

The victims of slavery and genocide were victims precisely because they deserved to be; it was their genetic destiny.

Laying this theory out for the world, Spencer (not Darwin) coined, in 1864, the phrase "survival of the fittest."[4]

By the 1870s and 1880s, as the myth of the cowboy had seized America's imagination, this new "scientific" theory injected a potent new poison into America's political and cultural bloodstream. Slavery and genocide weren't wrong; white-controlled America was simply making appropriate use of "beasts of burden" in the first instance and cleaning up the gene pool in the second.

The idea so infatuated well-educated Americans that Teddy Roosevelt himself, speaking to the Republican Club of New York City in 1905, said,

> *If in any community the level of intelligence, morality, and thrift among the colored men can be raised, it is, humanly speaking, sure that the same level among the whites will be raised to an even higher degree....*
>
> *The problem is so to adjust the relations between two races of different ethnic type that the rights of neither be abridged nor jeoparded; that the backward race be trained so that it may enter into the possession of true freedom ... while the forward race is enabled to preserve unharmed the high civilization wrought out by its forefathers.*[5]

Earlier in his life, Roosevelt had been more blunt: "I don't go so far as to think that the only good Indian is the dead Indian," he said, "but I believe nine out of every ten are, and I shouldn't like to inquire too closely into the case of the tenth.

The most vicious cowboy has more moral principle than the average Indian."[6]

Roosevelt, an ardent defender of working white people, was much more skeptical about people of other races. From his 1902 letter in which he argued that any white couple who didn't have children was contributing to "race suicide"[7] to his boosterism of the Spanish-American War's expansion into the Philippines by saying that Filipinos were "Chinese half-breeds," he echoed the white rationalization for the extermination or subjugation of nonwhite peoples.

And the principal instruments of that subjugation, from the earliest days of the republic, were guns.

Teddy Roosevelt was also a deeply mythologized gun-slinger who benefited directly from the myth of the cowboy. Americans glorify Roosevelt for leading the Rough Riders in guerrilla warfare during the Spanish-American War. Roosevelt's Rough Riders borrowed their name from hunter and showman Buffalo Bill, who himself capitalized on the myth of the cowboy with an 1898 vaudeville show called "Buffalo Bill's Wild West and Congress of Rough Riders of the World."

President Woodrow Wilson so enthusiastically jumped on the bandwagon of eugenics—the "science" of racial purity—with American-government-produced eugenics posters rationalizing sterilizing "mentally retarded" whites and presumably (but not explicitly, although he did screen the KKK-recruiting film *Birth of a Nation* at the White House) all blacks, that Hitler reproduced the posters in the 1930s and used American and British eugenics thinking to justify his "cleansing" of Germany.

American presidents from Roosevelt to Wilson were buying into the tenets of Darwin's cousin Sir Francis Galton, the British father of the modern eugenics movement, which white people from South Africa to Russia to Norway to America echoed to justify their "white supremacy."

Here, then, is the storm within a storm.

We committed genocide on a scale never before seen in the world, principally aided by the superior technology of guns.

We established a system of slavery, largely enforced by armed slave patrols.

When outlaws and sociopathic murderers—many of them ex-Confederate soldiers who'd fought to preserve slavery—rampaged across the West, American media romanticized their gunslinging ability and elevated the gun into a sort of totem of power and protection, in the hands of the mythologized "noble American rebel."

And now, as white children are being murdered en masse in schools across the country, white America is finally paying attention.

There are solutions to this epidemic of gun violence and mass shootings, but they first require a clear-eyed reconciliation of America's past with its present.

CHAPTER 14

The Gunshot That Ended Reconstruction

If this country cannot be saved without giving up that principle
[of ending slavery] ... I would rather be
assassinated on this spot than to surrender it.

–Abraham Lincoln, speech in Independence Hall,
Philadelphia, Pennsylvania, February 22, 1861[1]

The Civil War was over. The South had surrendered, and Lincoln had broken the South into administrative sections under control of the Union Army.

Southerners hated the arrangement—just four years earlier they had seceded from the United States to fight for their states' rights to own slaves. And now, they had lost the war and lost their slaves. Adding insult to injury, many southern slave patrols were replaced with police forces that included freedmen.

For more than a century, the hierarchy of the South was clear: there were the unarmed slaves, and there were the well-armed white folk. Now, with the Union Army in charge and freedmen acting as law enforcement, the tables seemed to be turned.

In short, they felt their way of life was being taken away by northern elitists who didn't understand or respect the culture of the Old South.

John Wilkes Booth was an actor who also held strong loyalties to the South. A supporter of slavery, he'd joined the Richmond militia and witnessed the hanging of abolitionist John Brown in October 1859. He escaped fighting for the South in the Civil War because he'd accidentally shot himself in the thigh during an 1860 performance of *Hamlet*.[2]

In November 1863, he performed in a play called *The Marble Heart* in Ford's Theatre in Washington, DC; in the audience were President and Mrs. Lincoln. A few months later, in May 1864, Booth invested his entire life savings in an oil operation in western Pennsylvania; it later turned out he'd been swindled and he lost everything. Bitter, angry, and fully bought into the southern story that the Civil War was all about the evil bankers and investor class in the Northeast, Booth joined a small group of bitter Confederates in a conspiracy to kill Lincoln and decapitate his administration.

Thus, in April 1865, Booth shot President Abraham Lincoln in the back of the head while the president enjoyed the play *Our American Cousin* at Ford's Theatre. Booth then flung himself from the balcony, making his motives clear as he dramatically shouted "*Sic semper tyrannis!*" ("Thus always to tyrants!").

The event marked the first time a US president was assassinated. It also marked the end of any serious efforts to reconstruct the South and to ensure the safety and equality of millions of newly enfranchised freedmen.

The end of the Civil War and the passage of the 13th, 14th, and 15th Amendments marked the official end of slavery in American history—but not the end of white supremacy, or of the Old South's race-based hierarchy and its use of guns to enforce it.

CHAPTER 15

The Failure of Reconstruction and the Rise of the Klan

The white men were roused by a mere instinct of self-preservation until at last there had sprung into existence a great Ku Klux Klan, a veritable empire of the South, to protect the Southern country.

–President Woodrow Wilson, who screened the Klan recruiting film *Birth of a Nation* in the White House

Armed police forces and their predecessors throughout history have been the major institutions that define hierarchies in a given area. A prime example of this is how Irish immigrants in America began to be accepted as "white" in the early 20th century as urban police forces became staffed with Irish immigrants, while Italian immigrants (who mostly came to the US in large numbers a few generations later in the late 19th century) became a more noticeable "other" who could be blamed for crime and "general seediness" in a community.

Before the Civil War, law enforcement was an all-white matter in the South. During Reconstruction, the Union Army disbanded the slave patrols and created new police departments in the South—with emancipated black freedmen acting as police officers and justices of the peace. Reconstruction was turning the Old South on its head—but not for long.

By removing Lincoln from power, John Wilkes Booth succeeded in using his gun to end the aspects of Reconstruction that southerners found most egregious. The vice president, whom Lincoln had chosen in a misplaced burst of hope for national unity, was Andrew Johnson, a southern Democrat.

Not only was Johnson a fan of slavery and a slaveholder, but the first slave he had bought, early in his life, was a 14-year-old girl, Dolly, who bore him three children. This fact became widely known while Johnson was still a state senator, and he addressed it by saying that Dolly had explicitly *asked* him to buy her because, he said, "she liked my looks." It was a thin excuse, but more than enough for southerners.[1]

Johnson quickly issued a series of proclamations that allowed southern states to establish their own civil governments and set their own policies without interference from the North. This effectively ended the Union Army's role in governing the South.

Not surprisingly, southern states quickly removed freedmen from police forces and began implementing "black codes" to preserve white supremacy in the South.

We see a telling example of how the Civil War and Reconstruction ultimately failed in Portsmouth, Virginia. Sally Hadden writes in *Slave Patrols* about the rapid changes in Portsmouth between Union occupation in 1861 and just five years later in 1866.

*When the coastal city of Portsmouth, Virginia, fell
to the Union Army in 1861, the residents saw their first
African American policemen, chief of police, and justices
of the peace. Prior to 1861 no police force had existed in
Portsmouth; instead, patrollers had the same duties as
"policemen of today," according to Jan Pyatt, a former
slave interviewed in the 1930s. In 1866, when civic
elections were held again, Pyatt reported that "a mayor
was elected head of the city, and the colored policemen,
Justice of the Peace, and Chief of Police was done away
with. In their places, a [civilian] provost-marshal with a
white staff was appointed."[2]*

At the end of the war, it wasn't uncommon for a freedman
to own a gun. Many newly freed black Americans had served
in the Union Army, and the federal government, short on
money to pay these soldiers' full wages, allowed former soldiers to keep their guns instead.

Suddenly, in the South, former slaves were arming themselves under the same Second Amendment that southern
slave owners had used to prevent and suppress slave revolts
for the previous 100 years.

Freedmen weren't just arming themselves; they began
to drill with their weapons in public, which only fueled race-
based fears of "Negro risings."

It didn't take any time at all for white southerners to realize that if the race-based hierarchy of the Old South was to be
preserved, white people needed to be the only armed people.

Hadden reports that "the occasional discovery of a cache of arms confirmed the worst fears and intensified the campaign to disarm the black population."[3]

As Adam Winkler wrote in the *New Republic* in 2013, "Within months of the surrender at Appomattox, recalcitrant white racists committed to the reestablishment of white supremacy determined to take those guns away from blacks. States in the South passed the Black Codes, which barred the freedmen from possessing guns. . . . To enforce these laws, racists began to form posses that would go out at night in large groups, generally wearing disguises, and terrorize black homes, seizing every gun they could find."[4]

In the Cape Fear region of North Carolina, Sally Hadden points out, the "county police" armed themselves to disarm freedmen and search for guns in the homes of black American citizens, in violation of the Fourth Amendment of the US Constitution.

In 1866, the same year that the mayor of Portsmouth, Virginia, purged the city's law enforcement ranks of freedmen, Governor Perry of South Carolina declared that militia organizations were "charged with the police and patrol duty of the country." Perry's decree, along with innumerable "black codes," was invalidated by Congress. But federal invalidation didn't stop white supremacists across the South from banding together to raid homes and disarm black Americans.

Police forces in the South adopted militaristic techniques that nearly every Southern male had learned while fighting for the Confederacy over the course of the Civil War.

While police departments in the South served to pre-serve the hierarchy of the Old South within the context of a post-slavery legal system, bands of posses and lynch mobs served to preserve the hierarchy of the Old South while ignoring completely any changes to the law.

A dramatized example of this is found in the Coen brothers' film *O Brother, Where Art Thou?* where the protagonists, facing three ropes and their own shallow-dug graves, tell their lynchers, "You can't do this—we just been pardoned! By the governor himself! . . . It went out on the radio!"

The characters' pleas are met with the simple statement, "Is that right? Too bad we don't have a radio." Similarly, in the more rural areas of the post-bellum South, federal and even state laws were meaningless and lacked any real local enforcement.

Black Americans often encountered even more brutality in the postwar South than they had as chattel slaves, Hadden notes, because "as slaves, bondsmen had been protected from patrollers by their masters, who (for paternalistic or material-istic reasons) did not wish to have their 'property' damaged by roving slave patrols."[5]

Southern posses and lynch mobs made sure that black Americans were intimidated and terrorized into staying sub-missive to their former owners and overseers, regardless of any new laws.

These roving bands didn't just search the homes of black Americans for guns; they were also looking for any "stolen property," a designation frequently applied to any goods in a freedman's possession, regardless of how the freedman had acquired it.

"Naturally," Hadden explains, "the stolen goods often ended up in the hands of county police who retrieved them but did not necessarily return them to their white, allegedly rightful, owners." (Today's police forces echo this practice with "civil asset forfeiture," a situation whereby police can simply seize someone's property without filing criminal charges against the person.)

At first, there were many of these posses across the South, which identified themselves with a variety of names: in Alabama there was the Black Cavalry, in Louisiana there were the Knights of the White Camellia, and in Texas there were the Knights of the Rising Sun, among countless others across the former Confederacy.[6]

Eventually all the groups became known simply as the Ku Klux Klan.

CHAPTER 16

Racists Turn Open Carry into the New White Hood

Whoever has experienced the power and the unrestrained ability to humiliate another human being automatically loses his own sensations. Tyranny is a habit, it has its own organic life, it develops finally into a disease. The habit can kill and coarsen the very best man or woman to the level of a beast. Blood and power intoxicate . . . the return of the human dignity, repentance, and regeneration becomes almost impossible.

–Fyodor Dostoyevsky, *The House of the Dead*

For decades after the failure of Reconstruction, Klan members in white hoods commonly showed up at southern polling places to intimidate black Americans. Through intimidation, white racists in the South could suppress black voter turnout and discourage votes for radical Republicans who wanted to see the South transformed away from its slaveholding roots. Intimidating voters was a way for the Klan and other racists to guarantee that the racist foundations of the American South were never seriously threatened.

In November 2016 there were no hooded figures at polling places, but there were plenty of white gun owners hanging around and brandishing their guns right out in the open. CNN described one such scene in Loudoun, Virginia, in November 2016:

> *A Trump supporter showed up to a Loudoun County polling station in Virginia, sporting a handgun in his waistband as he offered sample Republican ballots to voters outside.*
>
> *"And as a voter, I felt intimidated," Erika Cotti told CNN. "As my son and I walked away, I heard the man with the gun say . . . you're voting for Crooked Hillary."*
>
> *But elections officials say the man broke no laws, as Virginia is an open carry state—meaning that individuals are generally allowed to carry an unconcealed weapon in public.*[1]

Considering the racist and genocidal history of the Second Amendment and gun culture in America, it's hardly surprising that open carry has become the new white hood.

On August 11, 2017, thousands of white supremacists streamed into Charlottesville, Virginia. They were there to protest the removal of a statue of Confederate general Robert E. Lee from Charlottesville's Emancipation Park. Many of the white supremacists were armed with AR-15-style rifles along with tactical military and police gear.

It's not a coincidence that gun-toting white supremacists rallied in 2017 to protect a statue of Robert E. Lee. Robert E. Lee's claim to fame is that he was the general who led a traitorous revolt against the United States to preserve slavery in the South. As we've seen, the Second Amendment was ratified to enable genocide and to preserve slavery.

And the Civil War was fought, explicitly, to preserve slavery in the South. The South Carolina articles of secession laid it out clearly:

> The right of property in slaves was recognized by giving to free persons distinct political rights, by giving them the right to represent, and burthening them with direct taxes for three-fifths of their slaves; by authorizing the importation of slaves for twenty years; and by stipulating for the rendition of fugitives from labor.
>
> We affirm that these ends for which this Government was instituted have been defeated, and the Government itself has been made destructive of them by the action of the non-slaveholding States. Those States have assume the right of deciding upon the propriety of our domestic institutions; and have denied the rights of property established in fifteen of the States and recognized by the Constitution; they have denounced as sinful the institution of slavery; they have permitted open establishment among them of societies, whose avowed object is to disturb the peace and to eloign the property of the citizens of other States. They have encouraged and assisted thousands of our slaves to leave their homes; and those who remain, have been incited by emissaries, books and pictures to servile insurrection.[2]

Similar language can be found in the secession documents of the other southern states. Georgia, for example, proclaimed the following:

For the last ten years we have had numerous and serious causes of complaint against our non-slave-holding confederate States with reference to the subject of African slavery. They have endeavored to weaken our security, to disturb our domestic peace and tranquility, and persistently refused to comply with their express constitutional obligations to us in reference to that property, and by the use of their power in the Federal Government have striven to deprive us of an equal enjoyment of the common Territories of the Republic.

This hostile policy of our confederates has been pursued with every circumstance of aggravation which could arouse the passions and excite the hatred of our people, and has placed the two sections of the Union for many years past in the condition of virtual civil war. Our people, still attached to the Union from habit and national traditions, and averse to change, hoped that time, reason, and argument would bring, if not redress, at least exemption from further insults, injuries, and dangers. Recent events have fully dissipated all such hopes and demonstrated the necessity of separation.[3]

Probably not entirely unaware of the history of the region, the heavily militarized police of Charlottesville responded calmly to the mob of armed white supremacists. This was, again not coincidentally, in sharp contrast to the police response to protesters who had demanded justice for Freddie Gray in Baltimore, Maryland, two years earlier in 2015. Or three years earlier in Ferguson, Missouri, in 2014.

The police response in Charlottesville makes sense considering that police departments in the South are descended from slave patrols. The "antifascist protesters" in Charlottesville were reactionary, the police thought, expressing "Northern sentiments," and were protesting at a statue of a Confederate general, who'd fought to preserve the institution of slavery and, by extension, the institution of the slave patrol, from which modern American police departments, in many cases, descended.

Despite the abundance of guns and high tensions, the Charlottesville rally did not end with anyone being shot. It ended when James Fields Jr., a member of the alt-right, crashed his car through the crowd, injuring several counterprotesters and killing antifascist protester Heather Heyer.

There's need to wonder what would happen if Black Lives Matter activists organized, armed themselves with rifles, and marched the streets in any city or town across the country. The media have shown many recent instances of what happens when black Americans arm themselves and organize.

In 2018, members of the Baltimore Police were found to have carried BB guns with them to plant on black suspects in case the police "accidentally hit somebody or got into a shootout, so we could plant them."[4]

By planting a gun on a black American, the police could plausibly claim that they felt endangered, even if the police shooting was completely unjustified. In the case of Tamir Rice, police shot 12-year-old Tamir Rice to death in Cleveland, Ohio—because he was holding a BB gun in a park and someone called the police.[5] Even when it comes to toy BB guns or airsoft guns (like BB guns but with plastic balls), black Americans face potentially lethal consequences for carrying them in public.

In another case in March 2018, Stephon Clark was shot to death in his grandmother's backyard for holding a cellphone in a manner that police claim looked like he was brandishing a gun.[6]

In the 150 years since the Civil War, black Americans have been repeatedly disarmed by white authorities or killed when they attempted to exercise their Second Amendment rights. As with so many other things in America, history shows that the Second Amendment has never been "color-blind."

Actions on gun control have been swift when the people exercising their Second Amendment rights were black. Likewise, when a citizen has been killed while legally carrying a gun, the NRA has been deafeningly silent if that citizen is black.

In July 2016, a black man named Philando Castile was pulled over by the police in Minnesota, and he explained to the police officer that he had both a gun and a concealed carry permit and was going to get the permit out of his wallet. As he reached into his back pocket, as his girlfriend video-recorded the bloody incident, the police officer opened fire, killing Castile. Just months before, another African-American concealed carry permit holder, Mark Hughes, was shot to death by Dallas police who said he "looked like" a man wanted for terrorizing the neighborhood with an AR-15. The NRA said and did virtually nothing about either killing.

This double standard has allowed white supremacists to rally into motley groups that are clearly identified by one salient characteristic: they are armed, frequently with rifles, sidearms, and body armor . . . and are white.

CHAPTER 17

Copwatching and Its Connection to Gun Control

Yes, we do defend our office as we do defend our homes.
This is a constitutional right everybody has, and nothing's
funny about that. The only reason they get mad at the
Black Panther Party when you do it is for the simple reason
that we're political.

–Black Panther leader Fred Hampton, who was murdered in his sleep by the Chicago police and the FBI, December 4, 1969

More than anything else, the debate over the Second Amendment and guns has revolved around race and profits.

While usually framed as "sportsmen" and "self-defense" issues, neither, in fact, has been a primary animating force within the politics of the promotion of gun ownership and the relaxing of gun-control laws. The decisions, by both state and federal governments, have, in almost every case, had far more to do with race or money.

California in the 1960s, for example, and its governor Ronald Reagan were largely in favor of the ability of anybody who wanted to own a gun not only to own that gun but also to carry and wave it around in public, even if it was loaded.

But the first major modern-era rumblings of a white freak-out about black people owning and carrying guns began in a big way in February 1967.

That month, Bobby Seale and Huey Newton walked out of the Black Panthers' office in Oakland with, as Seale recounted in his book *Seize the Time*, a .45 pistol, a .357 pistol, "a couple of M-1" assault weapons, and "three or four shotguns."[1]

As they walked to their car and got in, a police car drove by. Within minutes, police surrounded them.

Sitting in their car, Newton gave his driver's license to the first police officer to walk up to the door and demand it, and, as Seale wrote, "Huey had a big M-1 sitting to his right with his hand on it. I had this 9mm sitting beside me, and Huey had this M-1 at his side." There were four other Black Panthers in the back seat, including Bobby Hutton.

"Can I see that pistol there?" one of the police asked Newton, according to Seale.

Pointing first to his pistol and then to the rifle, Newton replied, "No, you can't see the pistol, nor this [pointing to his rifle], and I don't want you to look at it. You don't have to look at it."

After some back-and-forth with the police, Newton, who'd taken law classes in San Francisco, said, "We have a constitutional right to carry the guns, anyway."

Seale writes that Newton stepped out of the car with the M-1 in his hand and jacked a round into the chamber as the police backed up.

"Who do you think you are, anyway?" Newton asked the police.

Another couple of cops were urging the growing crowd around the car to disperse, and Newton yelled out to the crowd, "You have a right to observe an officer carrying out his duty. You have a right to. As long as you stand a reasonable distance away, and you *are* a reasonable distance. *Don't go anywhere.*"

Newton then proceeded to call the officer interrogating him a "low-life scurvy swine" and "a sharecropper from racist Georgia." He added, "If you draw that gun, I'll shoot you and blow your brains out!"

The cop accused him of "turning the Constitution around," but Newton held his ground. He continued to berate the cops until they finally left.

That, Seale wrote in *Seize the Time*, was when he realized that Huey Newton was "the baddest motherf---er around."

That confrontation led the Black Panthers to form what they called Copwatch Patrols, traveling around the streets of first Oakland and then other cities with police scanners, showing up anytime police performed stops on people in black neighborhoods.

The stories are well known, and one could arguably draw a direct line from the Panthers' surveillance of police to the many video captures in the second decade of the 2000s that have shown so many unarmed black men and women being killed by police officers.

Newton and Seale cranked up the volume a few months later, on May 2, 1967, and immediately got the governor's attention.

Ronald Reagan was preparing to meet and share lunch with a group of eighth-graders visiting the state capitol when Newton, Seale, and nearly 30 other Black Panthers showed up.

Armed with everything from pistols to 12-gauge shotguns, Seale pulled out a prepared statement and read it to the students and people in front of the capitol: "The American people in general and the black people in particular must take careful note of the racist California legislature aimed at keeping the black people disarmed and powerless. Black people have begged, prayed, petitioned, demonstrated, and everything else to get the racist power structure of America to right the wrongs which have historically been perpetuated against black people. The time has come for black people to arm themselves against this terror before it is too late."[2]

Then they climbed the steps to the capitol building and walked right in, fully loaded guns and rifles in their hands.

Reagan and the white California legislators freaked out.

"There's no reason why on the street today a citizen should be carrying loaded weapons," Reagan said later that afternoon.

Shortly thereafter, Republican assemblyman Don Mulford of Oakland, with bipartisan support, introduced into the California State Assembly a law, later known as the Mulford Act (AB-1591), to ban people in California from carrying loaded weapons in public.[3] It was enthusiastically signed into law by Reagan on July 28.

Gun control, it seems, was just fine with Reagan and his white legislator friends so long as it was first applied to uppity black people.

Over the next decade, state after state passed gun-control laws like California's, as well as a federal law, until May 1977, according to Adam Winkler in his book *Gunfight*.[4]

That month saw the takeover of the NRA by Harlon Carter, a lobbyist for the NRA's Institute for Legislative Action. The takeover was in response to the decision by the NRA's board to move the group's headquarters from Washington, DC, to Colorado Springs, Colorado, then a hotbed of gun activity and publications.

Alarmed that the NRA was going to abandon their lobbying efforts, Carter, most likely with the help of weapons manufacturers, was elected VP of the NRA and pushed to keep the organization in DC, where he could lobby Congress for laxer gun controls.

His side won, and the interests of the gun manufacturers have, apparently, driven the major behaviors of the NRA ever since.

The desire to disarm black people, and the desire to sell more guns, were seemingly in direct conflict.

The solution that American law enforcement has chosen for centuries is to selectively kill black gun owners while ignoring white gun owners, even when they point their weapons at federal officers, as supporters of Cliven Bundy infamously did in 2014.[5]

As Mara H. Gottfried wrote for the Minneapolis–St. Paul *Twin Cities Pioneer Press* on July 7, 2016, "The death of 32-year-old Philando Castile appears to mark the first time a

Minnesota permit-to-carry holder had been shot by police at least since the current permit law took effect in 2003."[6]

Officer Jeronimo Yanez, who shot and killed Castile, was acquitted by a jury in June 2017.

Castile had not threatened Yanez and had not pointed his weapon at him; to the contrary, when first stopped, he told the officer, using the technique suggested by the NRA in numerous venues, that he had a licensed firearm in the car with him.[7]

Apparently, since the days when Reagan's California established rules for carrying loaded weapons, those rules of behavior apply only to white people who are licensed to carry.

CHAPTER 18

One Sunny August Day in Texas

I love her dearly. . . . I cannot rationally pinpoint any specific reason for doing this.

—Charles Whitman, in a note he left after murdering
his mother on the day of his mass-shooting spree,
August 1, 1966

At first, only Charles Whitman knew what was happening.

Claire James was a freshman at the University of Texas and was one of the first people whom Whitman shot from his perch in the University of Texas clock tower. Fifty years after Whitman shot James in America's first civilian mass shooting, she told *Texas Monthly* about how she had become one of America's first mass-shooting victims:

> We were walking across the South Mall, holding hands, when all of a sudden I felt like I'd stepped on a live wire, like I'd been electrocuted. I was eight months pregnant at the time. Tom said, "Baby—" and reached out for me. And then he was hit.
>
> Tom never said another word. I was lying next to him on the pavement, and I called out to him, but I knew he was dead. The shock was so great that I didn't feel pain; it felt more like something really heavy was

pressing down on me. A conservative-looking guy in
a suit walked by, and I yelled at him, "Please, get a
doctor! Please!" even though I still didn't understand
what was happening. He looked annoyed and said,
"Get up! What do you think you're doing?" I think he
thought it was guerrilla theater, because we had started
doing things like that to bring attention to the war in
Vietnam.[1]

Other bystanders thought the bangs were coming from
nearby construction.

In 1986, William Helmer wrote in *Texas Monthly* about
his experience watching Whitman methodically shoot one
person after another:

Walking from the old journalism building on
Twenty-fourth Street to the Union to get a sandwich
for lunch, I could hear loud reports that had the boom,
snap *quality of rifle shots. They were coming from*
the vicinity of the Main Building, but I didn't see any
unusual activity there and shrugged them off as the
sounds of a nail-driving gun, which had been periodi-
cally banging away on a construction project there. . . .

I was still operating on the nail-gun theory when
some students standing behind a pillar of the Academic
Center started shouting something about a guy on the
Tower shooting people and how I should get moving. My
first response was to resent being yelled at, so I just stood
there in the middle of a grassy inner-drive area, squinting

*up at the Tower's northwest corner. Sure enough, I could
see a gun barrel poke out over the parapet and emit
smoke, followed an instant later by the boom I had been
hearing. Now the computer was working a lot faster but
still coming up with a bad readout:* Just look at that!
There's some fool up there with a rifle, trying to get
himself in one hell of a lot of trouble! *From my angle,
it didn't look like the man was shooting downward, but
was trying to create a commotion.*[2]

Helmer's response was understandable—there had never
been a mass shooting of this scale on American soil, and certainly nowhere as public as a university campus. Soon after,
the full gravity of the situation sunk in for Helmer, and he
writes about the moments when he was thrown over the line
from observer to emergency responder and victim in Whitman's massacre:

*I could see the sniper fairly well; he would lean out
over the parapet, bring the rifle to bear on target, fire,
tip the weapon up as he worked the action, then walk
quickly to another point and do the same thing. It must
have been about that time that he hit an electrician
next to his truck at Twentieth Street and University
Avenue, a quarter of a mile away. It was about that
time, too, that the Tower clock started chiming and
then, with cold-blooded indifference, tolled the noon
hour. And it must have been only moments after those
echoes died that the sniper, evidently firing through one*

of the Tower's drain spouts, put a shot through the open window where the four of us stood gawking.

The bullet struck the edge of the window opening in front of the girl's face like an exploding stick of dynamite, filling the stairwell with glass, splinters, bullet fragments, and concrete dust. . . . I started crawling over to her, and my left hand slipped so that I partly fell forward into blood that was rapidly covering the floor of the stairwell. The blood wasn't hers; the bullet had fragmented, and a large chunk of it had pierced the right forearm of the guy on my side of the window. It had hit an artery that now, as he lay partly on his side, was pumping out blood in rapid squirts about three inches high.

It's strange what happens to time in situations like this. All motion slowed down and became dreamlike. . . . I could still hear the girl's sobbing, and I could hear my own voice, squawking for someone to give me a handkerchief. The shooting victim used his good arm to pull one from his back pocket and hand it to me. . . .

[W]hile washing up in the basement men's room, I found that what looked like a shaving cut in my neck held a piece of the bullet's copper jacket, not much bigger than a pinhead. Realizing that that could have been the large chunk of bullet made it hard to breathe for a little while.

Whitman was armed to the teeth, with three rifles, four pistols, and more than 700 rounds of ammunition. He had pur-chased a 12-gauge shotgun and an M1 carbine I the morning after he killed his wife and mother. According to *Mass Murderers* (Time-Life Books), when Whitman purchased the M1 carbine and eight boxes of ammunition, he told the cashier that he planned to hunt wild hogs.[3]

The day after the shooting, the *Waco News-Tribune* published the matter-of-fact headline "Sniper Atop UT Tower Kills 12, Wounds 31; Mother, Wife Found Dead in Their Homes." Below that headline, the unnamed *American Austin* reporter described Whitman as "a good son, a top Boy Scout, an excellent Marine, an honor student, a hard worker, a fine scout master, a handsome man, a wonderful friend to all who knew him—and an expert sniper."[4]

But only one of those descriptors ("an expert sniper") is relevant to Whitman's role in America's first civilian mass shooting. And while few knew it at the time, the shooting at the University of Texas set a pattern for many more.

The pattern goes beyond "a man gets a gun and tries to kill people." It extends into the factors leading up to such a drastic course of action, and it extends into how the media covers "mass shootings" versus "acts of terrorism."

Across many of the deadliest mass shootings in America, there is a similar pattern over the last half century of mass shootings. America's deadliest civilian mass shootings have all occurred since 1960, and most of them were committed by young white men: the University of Texas shooting (1966); the San Ysidro, California, McDonald's massacre (1984); the Edmond, Oklahoma, post office shooting (1986); the Luby's Cafeteria massacre in Killeen, Texas (1991); the Aurora,

Colorado, movie theater shooting (2012); the Sutherland Springs, Texas, church shooting (2017); the Las Vegas shooting (2017); and the school shootings at Columbine, Colorado (1999), Sandy Hook, Connecticut (2012), and Marjory Stoneman Douglas High School in Parkland, Florida (2018).

These shootings happened at different times in different places across the country, but in all of these shootings there are a few consistent patterns:

1. the shooter was white and male, who felt generally betrayed and alienated by society, and empowered by guns;

2. the shooter didn't seem to have precise targets and was out to use his guns to kill indiscriminately; and

3. in the aftermath of the terroristic act, the shooter's actions were strangely explained away. He was described as a "lone wolf," probably mentally ill, and in the aftermath of a terroristic act, his biography was probed to find redeeming qualities. (Charles Whitman's behavior has often been controversially explained away as the result of a brain tumor.[5])

Mass shootings don't occur in a vacuum. Gun advocates and their detractors alike can agree that guns represent a sense of power. It is easy to say that mass shooters are "losers" and they lash out at being "bullied." From there, it becomes clear why they take up guns: throughout history, guns have represented power and control.

But there's something missing from this analysis: why are so many white men feeling like losers who perceive themselves as both alienated and bullied by society?

What is missed in a discussion limited to mental illness and lone wolves are the exploitatively political and social contexts that make individuals feel like lone wolves in America. Understanding those contexts is key to understanding why most (but not all) people who commit mass shootings in America are white males, and why white males have committed mass shootings more and more frequently over the last half century.

CHAPTER 19

1966: A Turning Point in America's Gun Culture

There are no free and democratic and wealthy countries in the world that have our rate of gun violence.

–E. J. Dionne, *PBS NewsHour*

In October 2017, Stephen Paddock rained down bullets on concertgoers at the Route 91 Harvest music festival on the Las Vegas Strip. By the time Paddock shot himself and ended the massacre, he had shot 58 people to death and injured 851 others.

Following the massacre, criminologist Grant Duwe documented for the *Washington Post* that between 1916 and 1966, there had been only 25 mass public shootings.[1]

Since Charles Whitman climbed the University of Texas clock tower in 1966, well over 1,000 people have been killed in more than 150 public mass shootings. That figure includes the February 14, 2018, mass shooting at Marjory Stoneman Douglas High School.[2] By the time you read this book, those figures will certainly be even higher.

Many authors use the University of Texas clock tower shooting in 1966 to mark a sharp divide in American history in terms of gun violence. But Whitman's massacre wasn't a lone incident that set the United States on course to be the only developed country on earth where public mass shootings regularly occur.

In late 1966, the United States was in the throes of social transformation:

- More and more young people were turning out to protest the illegal war in Vietnam and to speak out against what they saw as the sacrifice of an entire generation in a senseless war-for-profit.

- Civil rights activist James Meredith was shot by a white gunman while Meredith marched to high-light ongoing racism in the South despite the Civil Rights Act of 1964 and the Voting Rights Act of 1965. While Meredith and other civil rights activists felt that social transformation was happening too slowly, southern white racists felt that their world was being turned upside down.

- A reactionary B-movie-actor-turned-politician named Ronald Reagan was elected governor of California, promising to "send the welfare bums back to work" and to "clean up the mess at Berkeley."[3]

Between the Vietnam War and racist gun violence, America was already steeped in gun violence before 1966, but not the same type of mass killings that we've seen since August 1966. America's racist gun culture had been well established throughout American history.

As of this writing, October 2018 was a high-water mark for white male terror in America. Donald Trump was on the campaign trail for Republicans in the lead-up to the midterm elections, and he spent much of the month stoking fears about a migrant "caravan" approaching the United States from Central America. But while Trump stoked fear about a faceless nonwhite horde approaching the United States, white nationalists and anti-Semites repeatedly made headlines for various acts of terror.

On October 15, Portland, Oregon, Mayor Ted Wheeler announced that Portland police had found a "cache of firearms" during an extreme-right-wing rally in August. A group called Patriot Prayer had hosted the march for "law and order," harking back to the tried-and-true southern-strategy dog whistle. The event had national attention from the moment it was announced, as citizens in Portland organized for a counterprotest. The August protest sparked a brief national debate about political violence; a minute-long melee had broken out between the two groups before police intervened.

Wheeler's announcement may have surprised some, especially since two months had passed and no one had reported on the weapons cache, even though police reportedly discovered the stockpiled weapons before the event. Wheeler told reporters, "The Portland Police Bureau discovered individuals who positioned themselves on a rooftop parking structure in downtown Portland with a cache of firearms."[4]

According to police, the guns were unloaded, one was disassembled, and the men all had concealed carry permits, so the police simply told them to put the guns in a locked container, and then they left them alone. It's hard to imagine a similar outcome if police had found a group of Black Lives Matter activists with a stash of guns, unloaded or otherwise, in a parking garage.

Later in October 2018, a bomb arrived at the home of billionaire George Soros. Soros was likely targeted because he was a big supporter of Democratic causes and a survivor of the Holocaust. That made him the perfect person for right-wing conspiracy theorists, anti-Semites, and white nationalists to focus on as the ultimate bad guy. Soros had been blamed for everything from "inventing global warming" to funding the migrant "caravan" that dominated much of the news cycle in October 2018.

On October 26, police arrested Cesar Sayoc, an avowed Trump supporter from Florida. In total he mailed 13 packages to high-profile Democrats, including former Attorney General Eric Holder and actor and activist Robert De Niro, along with former Secretary of State Hillary Clinton and former President Barack Obama. He also mailed one package to CNN.

The thread tying all of the targets together was that they were all people whom Trump had insulted or otherwise disparaged during his rallies. Trump, of course, denied any influence on Sayoc's actions, even though Trump offered to pay his supporters' legal fees for assaulting protesters[5] and even suggested that "the Second Amendment people" might have somehow stopped Hillary Clinton if she had won the 2016 election.[6]

On October 27, an anti-Semite named Robert Bowers shot 11 people to death in the Tree of Life synagogue in Pittsburgh, Pennsylvania. In the weeks leading up to Bowers's anti-Semitic attack, he had posted online about his handgun collection, which included 21 registered handguns. He also spent time online blaming Jewish people for supporting the migrant caravan, much like what Cesar Sayoc seemed to believe.

Minutes before he entered the synagogue, Bowers posted online, "I can't sit by and watch my people get slaughtered. Screw your optics, I'm going in."[7]

All these headlines dwarfed the defacing of a string of synagogues with anti-Semitic graffiti over the course of October, from California[8] to Brooklyn.[9]

On November 2, a 40-year-old white man named Scott Beierle entered a yoga studio in Tallahassee, Florida, and shot six people, killing two women before he killed himself. In the aftermath of the shooting, reporters found that Beierle had posted a series of online videos espousing misogyny and blaming women who refused to sleep with him or date him, echoing decades of American men who have picked up guns and committed murder in the pursuit of "masculinity."[10]

These headlines represent a growing trend of right-wing male violence in America. As the Center for Strategic & International Studies (CSIS) notes, "Terrorist attacks by right-wing extremists in the United States have increased. Between 2007 and 2011, the number of such attacks was five or less per year. They then rose to 14 in 2012; continued at a similar level between 2012 and 2016, with a mean of 11 attacks and a median of 13 attacks; and then jumped to 31 in 2017. FBI arrests of right-wing extremists also increased in 2018."[11]

In that same report, CSIS states that the weapons of choice for right-wing terrorist attacks are firearms: 37 percent of right-wing attacks between 2007 and 2017 were committed with firearms. The second-most-common weapons for right-wing extremists are incendiary devices, such as pipe bombs, accounting for 35 percent of right-wing attacks over the same decade.[12]

As of this writing, the murder of a dozen people at the Borderline Bar & Grill in Thousand Oaks, California, on November 7, 2018, was the 307th mass shooting of the year. *USA Today* reported that 328 people were killed, 1,251 were injured, and thousands of families were shattered.

USA Today noted that the California mass shooting "came during three weeks of hate and terror that have jolted the country [in the run-up to the 2018 midterm elections]: a bloodbath at a synagogue in Pittsburgh that left 11 elderly people dead and a series of 16 pipe bombs mailed to prominent Democrats, CNN and critics of President Donald Trump."[13]

But in the long run, it was the southern-strategy race-baiting of Richard Nixon; the reactionary economics of Ronald Reagan; and the hate-driven "othering" of Mexicans, African-Americans, and Muslims by Donald Trump that collectively transformed America economically and socially.

CHAPTER 20

Guns, Militarism, and the War on Drugs

The War on Drugs employs millions—politicians, bureaucrats, policemen, and now the military—that probably couldn't find a place for their dubious talents in a free market, unless they were to sell pencils from a tin cup on street corners.

– Science-fiction author and political activist L. Neil Smith

In 2012, a Kansas SWAT team carrying weapons of war worthy of an operation against ISIS raided the home of Robert and Addie Harte and tore their house apart looking for evidence of a major marijuana-growing operation.

The investigation began when a state trooper stationed at a gardening supply store (yes, they had the gardening store staked out!) spotted Robert Harte and his son purchasing supplies to grow hydroponic tomatoes.

According to the *Washington Post*, having seen the Hartes buying hydroponic growing accessories, the Johnson County Sheriff's Department started investigating the Harte family.[1]

They searched the family's trash and found "saturated plant material" that supposedly tested positive for THC, the active chemical in marijuana.

But in reality, Mrs. Harte is a tea drinker, and that wet plant matter was nothing more than used tea leaves; the SWAT raid, when the wet tea was retested, had turned up nothing.

The family sued for false arrest and intimidation, but a federal judge dismissed the family's lawsuit against the police, saying that the sheriffs had probable cause based on the garden store purchase and old tea leaves.

But the Hartes aren't the average targets of this kind of drug sting, and one sheriff actually boasted after the raid that the operation was so unusual because they'd shut down a drug operation that was run by an "average family" in a "good neighborhood," all coded language for "middle-class white people."

Aside from the fact that the Hartes weren't actually doing anything illegal, the sheriff unwittingly showed just how exceptional it was that the family was a target at all.

Because the war on drugs has never been about drugs.

The war on drugs, since Richard Nixon declared it, has been about controlling political power by breaking up black communities and the dissident left. The people who were involved, the architects and the leaders in the war on drugs, admitted it and even bragged about it.

Before he died, Nixon counsel and former assistant to the president John Ehrlichman told author Dan Baum,

> *The Nixon campaign in 1968, and the Nixon
> White House after that, had two enemies: the antiwar
> left and black people. You understand what I'm saying?
> We knew we couldn't make it illegal to be either against
> the war or black, but by getting the public to associate
> the hippies with marijuana and blacks with heroin, and
> then criminalizing both heavily, we could disrupt those*

*communities. We could arrest their leaders, raid their
homes, break up their meetings and vilify them night
after night on the evening news. Did we know we were
lying about the drugs? Of course we did.*[2]

The Nixon administration signed the Controlled Substances Act into law in 1970, officially codifying the war on drugs into federal law, and then used the war on drugs to help politically (and often physically) assassinate community leaders, and to fracture communities by removing individuals from society and throwing them in prison.

By 1973, more than 300,000 people were being arrested every year under the law, and a disproportionate number of those were African-Americans.

The plan went hand in hand with the Republican southern strategy, as former Republican strategist Lee Atwater described.[3]

Nixon and his advisers weren't the first to invent and promote a racist war on drugs, though, and use the armed power of the state to destroy US citizens' lives. Using drug enforcement as a way to oppress minority communities already had a 40-year precedent.

In the 1930s, Harry J. Anslinger served as the first commissioner of the US Treasury Department's Federal Bureau of Narcotics, which eventually became the Drug Enforcement Agency. Back then, he reportedly claimed, "There are 100,000 total marijuana smokers in the US, and most are Negroes, Hispanics, Filipinos and entertainers. Their Satanic music, jazz and swing result from marijuana use. This marijuana causes white women to seek sexual relations with Negroes, entertainers and any others."[4]

He also used explicit racist epithets in his diatribes, saying, "Reefer makes darkies think they're as good as white men."

The language had become subtler by the 1970s, but the ideas were the same.

According to the Justice Policy Institute, approximately 500,000 people were serving time for drug offenses in state and federal prisons and jails in 2008.[5] Unsurprisingly, the NAACP reports that 38 percent of people arrested for drug offenses are black, and 59 percent of drug offenders in state prisons are African-American (while blacks represent about 17 percent of the population).[6]

The war on drugs costs America tens of billions in federal and state tax dollars every year, and the only result has been millions of undue criminal convictions that have ruined lives, destroyed communities, and undermined democracy.[7]

Today, the genocide of Native Americans has settled into a slow simmer of malnutrition, poverty, and voter suppression; the enslavement of people of African descent has shifted from plantations to slums and prisons; and the modern police state constructed during the conquest era, the slavery era, and Reconstruction after the Civil War, and thrown into high gear in the 1970s with Nixon's war on drugs, is still alive and well.

All it requires to keep it in place is lots of guns.

CHAPTER 21

Heller: Reinterpreting the Second Amendment

*The Court would have us believe that over 200 years ago,
the Framers made a choice to limit the tools available to
elected officials wishing to regulate civilian uses of weapons,
and to authorize this Court to use the common-law process
of case-by-case judicial lawmaking to define the contours of
acceptable gun control policy. Absent compelling evidence that is
nowhere to be found in the Court's opinion, I could not possibly
conclude that the Framers made such a choice.*

–Justice John Paul Stevens's dissenting opinion in
District of Columbia v. Heller

The June 26, 2008, Supreme Court decision in the case of *District of Columbia v. Heller* was a pivotal turn in America's understanding of the Second Amendment. But it was also a substantial rewrite of the Second Amendment, both in detail and in its very history.

As the historical record clearly shows, that amendment was created to satisfy two constituencies and had virtually nothing to do with the *Heller* finding that there was an "individual right" to gun ownership in the United States. So who were the groups who pushed for this particular amendment to the brand-new Constitution?

The first was what would become the anti-Federalist faction, led by Jefferson, which was concerned that if the country maintained a standing army during times of peace, members of that army might conspire to overthrow the new government that the founders had just created (something that has happened frequently in history, around the world, from ancient times to today).

The second constituency was the representatives of the slave states, who were concerned that the Article I, Section 8, authority of the federal government to call up an army might end up freeing slaves in the process, and they wanted to protect their state militias, which were largely then known, in those slave states, as slave patrols.

But in 2008, in a squeaker 5–4 decision, Justice Antonin Scalia stretched logic and fantasy to the breaking point to "discover," for the first time in nearly 230 years, that there was a secret private right to gun ownership "in defense of hearth and home" buried deep within the Second Amendment.[1]

Scalia's first argument was that the Second Amendment's use of the phrase "right of the people" to keep and bear arms meant to give everybody in the US the largely unlimited right to gun ownership, just as the First and Fourth Amendments, respectively, protect *everybody's* right to free speech and privacy.

This was the first time in the nearly 230-year history of the United States that any court—or any branch of government, for that matter—had suggested such a thing. Thus, in the dissent written by Justice Stevens and joined by Justices Breyer, Souter, and Ginsberg, they noted that Scalia's new theory about the founders' intent was, essentially, nonsense made up to keep happy the hard right and the gun lobby that so richly supported the GOP.

"The centerpiece of the Court's textual argument," Stevens and his colleagues wrote, summarizing Scalia's argument, "is its insistence that the words 'the people' as used in the Second Amendment must have the same meaning, and protect the same class of individuals, as when they are used in the First and Fourth Amendments. According to the Court, in all three provisions—as well as the Constitution's preamble, section 2 of Article I, and the Tenth Amendment—'the term unambiguously refers to all members of the political community, not an unspecified subset.'"

Stevens then took apart Scalia's argument:

> But the Court itself reads the Second Amendment to protect a "subset" significantly narrower than the class of persons protected by the First and Fourth Amendments; when it finally drills down on the substantive meaning of the Second Amendment, the Court limits the protected class to "law-abiding, responsible citizens."
>
> But the class of persons protected by the First and Fourth Amendments is not so limited; for even felons (and presumably irresponsible citizens as well) may invoke the protections of those constitutional provisions. The Court offers no way to harmonize its conflicting pronouncements.

Scalia also argued, in the absence of any evidence whatsoever from the time of the amendment's ratification, that the

Second Amendment was passed to allow individuals to own guns for self-defense (which was the essence of the *Heller* case, as Washington, DC, had forbidden people from owning guns even for that reason), rather than a purely military/militia context.

Stevens et al., in their dissent (which, but for one Republican-appointed justice, would have been the majority decision), argued back,

> The stand-alone phrase "bear arms" most naturally conveys a military meaning unless the addition of a qualifying phrase signals that a different meaning is intended. When, as in this case, there is no such qualifier, the most natural meaning is the military one; and, in the absence of any qualifier, it is all the more appropriate to look to the preamble to confirm the natural meaning of the text.
>
> The Court's [Scalia's] objection is particularly puzzling in light of its own contention that the addition of the modifier "against" changes the meaning of "bear arms."

They added, quoting a previous Supreme Court decision on the topic,

> The phrase "bear Arms" also had at the time of the founding an idiomatic meaning that was significantly different from its natural meaning: to serve as a soldier, do military service, fight or to wage war. But it unequivocally bore that idiomatic meaning only when followed by the preposition "against." . . .

> *When each word in the text is given full effect, the Amendment is most naturally read to secure to the people a right to use and possess arms in conjunction with service in a well-regulated militia. So far as appears, no more than that was contemplated by its drafters or is encompassed within its terms. . . .*
>
> *Indeed, not a word in the constitutional text even arguably supports the Court's overwrought and novel description of the Second Amendment as "elevat[ing] above all other interests" "the right of law-abiding, responsible citizens to use arms in defense of hearth and home."*

Even a previous Supreme Court chief justice, Nixon appointee Warren Berger, called the idea that the Second Amendment conferred an "individual right" to gun ownership a lie. Explicitly, he said the idea being promoted back when he was on the Court was "a fraud on the American public."

An early draft of the Second Amendment shows this brightly: it included a conscientious-objector provision for Quakers, letting them opt out of the militia. It read, "A well regulated militia composed of the body of the people, being the best security of a free state, the right of the people to keep and bear arms shall not be infringed, but no one religiously scrupulous of bearing arms, shall be compelled to render military service in person."

In fact, through the entirety of James Madison's notes on the 1787 Constitutional Convention, when military service and gun ownership were extensively discussed and debated, there is not even one single reference to an individual right to own a gun "to defend hearth and home."[2] (It's interesting how Scalia used language similar to that in common usage in 1787 to invent his version of early American history: no doubt it caused many people to assume that it was a direct quote from one of America's Founders, when, in fact, no such phrase exists.)

A deep dive into the 1788 Convention in Virginia, where the state's legislature debated ratification of the Constitution, finds that debate took a huge sideways turn into editing what would be the 1791-ratified Bill of Rights, in part because "father of the Constitution" James Madison was a Virginian and representative of that state to the ratification convention.

The word "nation" was modified to "state" and the religious exemption was deleted, but there was, again, not a single word about a Second Amendment right to individual gun ownership, even to defend a home's fireplace (hearth) or relatives (home). Instead, Patrick Henry pontificated at length about the importance of protecting state militias, aka slave patrols, to defend his plantation and those of his fellow Virginia slavers from runaways and slave revolts.

Again the next year, in June 1798, when the Bill of Rights was being debated in the US House of Representatives prior to presenting it for final ratification by the states, the members of the House held extensive discussions about the need for each state to raise a militia and fund it themselves, and whether arms should be held at home or in an armory.[3]

They even debated the Quakers' religious exemption and finally agreed to include it in the Second Amendment—this was really more a debate about that century's version of a military draft—but there was not one single word spoken in the entire month of debate about "hearth," "home," or anything resembling an "individual right" to own a gun for hunting, sport, or self-defense.

Similarly, throughout the 19th century, gun control was widespread from cities on the East Coast to the Wild West. Tombstone, Arizona, for example, had a strict law that all guns had to be checked with and stored by either the sheriff or the Grand Hotel.[4] Wyatt Earp and Doc Holliday were outlaws, not heroes, until the fiction writers got hold of their story; both were charged with murder. The judge even "fined one of the victims $25 earlier that day for packing a pistol."[5]

So how did this "fraud on the American public" begin, and end up before the Supreme Court?

The story is, at its core, all about an industry willing to spend millions to protect its profits and a political party willing to frighten American gun owners for purely political purposes.

As Michael Waldman points out in a seminal and detailed 2014 article for Politico, as recently as 1972, Richard Nixon ran for reelection on a popular (90 percent) and Republican position of gun control, particularly over "cheap handguns."[6]

In 1980, however, Ronald Reagan was the first presidential candidate to be endorsed in the history of the NRA, in part because of his position that there should be no federal regulation of handguns. As the Republican Party platform said that year, "We believe the right of citizens to keep and bear arms must be preserved. Accordingly, we oppose federal registration of firearms."

But the NRA, taken over in the early '70s by hard-right/ libertarian ideologues, was just getting started. Seeing the reconsideration of the Second Amendment as their ticket to power and riches, the NRA began funding scholars and think tanks across the nation, looking for the magic bullet (no pun intended) that would give them and their manufacturers the absolute constitutional cudgel to use against the majority of the American public who favored reasonable gun control.

Their first argument was that the Second Amendment was passed, bizarrely, so that the early colonists could wage war against their own government just like they had the British, if that government ever became "destructive," to use the language of the Declaration of Independence:

> *That whenever any Form of Government becomes destructive of these ends, it is the Right of the People to alter or to abolish it, and to institute new Government, laying its foundation on such principles and organizing its powers in such form, as to them shall seem most likely to effect their Safety and Happiness. . . . [W]hen a long train of abuses and usurpations, pursuing invariably the same Object evinces a design to reduce them under absolute Despotism, it is their right, it is their duty, to throw off such Government, and to provide new Guards for their future security.*

The only major rebellion against the new United States government happened in 1787, when Daniel Shays led 4,000 armed men to Springfield, Massachusetts, to try to seize the armory to challenge the US government. Shays' Rebellion was put down by the Massachusetts militia, leading to charges of rebellion against hundreds, a death sentence for 18 men, and the hanging of two.

Nobody—literally not a single member of the founders or framers of the Constitution—suggested that they had a "Second Amendment right" to armed rebellion.

George Washington, who would later lead troops (as a sitting president, no less) to put down the 1794 Whiskey Rebellion, wrote to Henry Lee of Shays' Rebellion: "You talk, my good sir, of employing influence to appease the present tumults in Massachusetts. I know not where that influence is to be found, or, if attainable, that it would be a proper remedy for the disorders. Influence is not government. Let us have a government by which our lives, liberties, and properties will be secured, or let us know the worst at once."

Colonial history is littered with stories of smaller rebellions, all led by well-armed citizens wanting to rebel against their new government, and every one of them was successfully put down by members of the founding generation.

Nonetheless, the NRA was committed to promoting the idea that the founders actually wanted Americans to view their government with a jaundiced eye, ever ready to rise up in armed revolt. They advanced the "right of rebellion" as the rationale (with no substantial evidence whatsoever) so effectively that today, whenever I bring up gun control on my nationally syndicated radio show, people call in to promote the idea that they need their guns in case the government ever becomes "oppressive."

From there, their logic proceeded to the idea that in order to preserve the right to overthrow America's government (and to protect "hearth and home"), all Americans had an "individual right" to own the gun of their choice.

While there is no such language in the Constitution or Bill of Rights, and none of the founders ever endorsed such an idea at law, between NRA publications, op-eds, well-placed talking heads in the media, and the GOP's endorsement, the idea of this newly promoted "individual right" (the first time Waldman could find it mentioned was in 1960) in the Second Amendment became so entrenched in public consciousness that the American electorate wasn't shocked when it was "discovered" there by the Supreme Court in the *Heller* decision in 2008.

While that's the bad news of *Heller*, arguably the good news is that *Heller* also left intact the government's right to "reasonable" regulation of firearms.

Reasonable, of course, is determined by the times. While AR-15s, bump stocks, and cop-killing bullets were all deemed "reasonable" from the time of *Heller* until 2018, the nationwide eruption around the Parkland, Florida, mass murders has galvanized the country—particularly its young people— in a way that the world hasn't seen since the Port Arthur Massacre transformed Australia's gun laws.

There's hope.

Political Corruption Underwrites America's Gun-Control Nightmare

At bottom, the Court's opinion is thus a rejection of the common sense of the American people, who have recognized a need to prevent corporations from undermining self-government since the founding, and who have fought against the distinctive corrupting potential of corporate electioneering since the days of Theodore Roosevelt. It is a strange time to repudiate that common sense. While American democracy is imperfect, few outside the majority of this court would have thought its flaws included a dearth of corporate money in politics.

–Justice John Paul Stevens's dissent in *Citizens United*

Parkland shooting survivor and activist David Hogg once asked, when Sen. John McCain, R-Ariz., was still alive, why McCain had taken more than $7 million from the NRA (not to mention other millions that they and other "gun rights" groups spent supporting him indirectly).

McCain's answer, no doubt, would be the standard politician-speak these days: "They support me because they like my positions; I don't change my positions just to get their money." It's essentially what Sen. Marco Rubio, R-Fla., told the Parkland kids when he was confronted with a similar question.

And it's a nonsense answer, as everybody knows.

America has had an on-again, off-again relationship with political corruption that goes all the way back to the early years of this republic. Perhaps the highest level of corruption, outside of today, happened in the late 1800s, the tail end of the Gilded Age. ("Gilded," of course, refers to "gold coated or gold colored," an era that Donald Trump has tried so hard to bring back that he even replaced the curtains in the Oval Office with gold ones.)

One of the iconic stories from that era was that of William Clark, who died in 1925 with a net worth in excess, in today's money, of $4 billion. He was one of the richest men of his day, perhaps second only to John D. Rockefeller. And in 1899, Clark's story helped propel an era of political cleanup that reached its zenith with the presidency of progressive Republicans (that species no longer exists) Teddy Roosevelt and William Howard Taft.

Clark's scandal even led to the passage of the 17th Amendment, which let the people of the various states decide who would be their U.S. senators, instead of the state legislatures deciding, which was the case from 1789 until 1913, when that amendment was ratified.

By 1899, Clark owned pretty much every legislator of any consequence in Montana, as well as all but one newspaper in the state. Controlling both the news and the politicians, he figured they'd easily elect him to be the next U.S. senator from Montana. Congress later learned that he not only owned the legislators but in all probability stood outside the state house with a pocket full of $1,000 bills (literally: they weren't taken out of circulation until 1969 by Richard Nixon), each in a plain white envelope to hand out to every member who'd voted for him.[1]

When word reached Washington, DC, about the envelopes and the cash, the US Senate began an investigation into Clark, who told friends and aides, "I never bought a man who wasn't for sale."

Mark Twain wrote of Clark, "He is as rotten a human being as can be found anywhere under the flag; he is a shame to the American nation, and no one has helped to send him to the Senate who did not know that his proper place was the penitentiary, with a chain and ball on his legs."

State Senator Fred Whiteside, who owned the only non-Clark-owned newspaper in the state, the *Kalispell Bee*, led the big exposé of Clark's bribery. The rest of the Montana senators, however, ignored Whiteside and took Clark's money.[2]

The US Senate launched an investigation in 1899 and, sure enough, found out about the envelopes and numerous other bribes and emoluments offered to state legislators, and refused to seat him. The next year, Montana's corrupt governor appointed Clark to the Senate, and he served a full eight-year term.

Clark's story went national and became a rallying cry for clean-government advocates. In 1912, President Taft, after doubling the number of corporations being broken up by the Sherman Anti-Trust Act over what Roosevelt had done, championed the 17th Amendment (direct election of senators, something some Republicans today want to repeal) to prevent the kind of corruption that Clark represented from happening again.

Meanwhile, in Montana, while the state legislature was fighting reforms, the citizens put a measure on the state ballot of 1912 that would outlaw corporations from giving any money of any sort to politicians. That same year, Texas and other states passed similar legislation (the corrupt speaker of the House Tom DeLay, R-Texas, was prosecuted under that law).

Montana's anticorruption law, along with those of numerous other states, persisted until 2010,[3] when Justice Anthony Kennedy, writing for the five-vote majority on the US Supreme Court, declared in the *Citizens United* decision that in examining more than 100,000 pages of legal opinions, he could not find ". . . any direct examples of votes being exchanged for . . . expenditures. This confirms *Buckley*'s reasoning that independent expenditures do not lead to, or create the appearance of, quid pro quo corruption [*Buckley* is the 1976 decision that money equals free speech]. In fact, there is only scant evidence that independent expenditures even ingratiate. Ingratiation and access, in any event, are not corruption."[4]

The US Supreme Court, following on the 1976 *Buckley* case that grew straight out of the Powell Memo and was written in part by Justice Lewis Powell, turned the definitions of corruption upside down.[5]

That same year, the Court overturned the Montana law in the 2010 *American Tradition Partnership, Inc. v. Bullock* ruling,[6] essentially saying that money doesn't corrupt politicians, particularly if that money comes from corporations that can "inform" us about current issues (the basis of the *Citizens United* decision) or billionaires (who, apparently the right-wingers on the Court believe, obviously know what's best for the rest of us).

Thus, the reason the NRA can buy and own senators like McCain and Rubio (and Thom Tillis, R-N.C./$4 million; Cory Gardner, R-Colo./$3.8 million; Joni Ernst, R-Iowa/$3 million; and Rob Portman, R-Ohio/$3 million, who all presumably took money much faster and much more recently than even McCain) is because the Supreme Court has repeatedly said that corporate and billionaire money never corrupts politicians.[7] (The dissent in the *Citizens United* case is a must-read: it's truly mind-boggling and demonstrates beyond refutation how corrupted the right-wingers on the Court, particularly Scalia and Thomas—who regularly attended events put on by the Kochs—were by billionaire and corporate money.)[8]

So here America stands. The Supreme Court has ruled, essentially, that the NRA can own all the politicians they want and can dump unlimited amounts of poison into this nation's political bloodstream.

Meanwhile, angry white men who want to commit mass murder are free to buy and carry all the weaponry they can afford.

Gun-Control Activists Are Confronting Only the Tip of the Iceberg

I would like to have an ample fund to spread the light of Republicanism, but I am willing to undergo the disadvantage to make certain that in the future we shall reduce the power of money in politics for unworthy purposes.

–President William Howard Taft commenting on the 1907 Tillman Act, which banned corporate contributions to federal elections and was overturned by *Citizens United*

Activists struggle to fight for the climate, the rights of communities to be free of pollution from fracking or factory farms, the rights of citizens to health care and education, and dozens of other issues where the government has the ability to limit predatory corporate behavior. Unfortunately, because of corporate money, the federal government and many state governments are making things worse for humans and the earth while jacking up profits and tax cuts for corporations and billionaires.

But there are solutions. While Americans work hard to clean up America's gun problem—and the Parkland activists have highlighted the cause and encouraged the nation to take a chance to make real change happen now—there's also important work needed to get money out of politics.

It was financial corruption, after all, that got modern America in today's extreme gun mess in the first place; the history of the *Heller* decision is a horrible story of well-funded right-wing groups testing message after message until they found one that would stick with like-minded "conservatives" on the Supreme Court.

There are three big ways to overturn the power that billionaires and corporations have seized through their corruption of the Supreme Court.

The first way is to replace enough members of the Court to ensure a moderate or even progressive majority. This looked like a very real possibility in 2000, when George W. Bush lost the national vote to Al Gore by more than a half million votes and, according to a recount done by a consortium of newspapers, would have lost, as the *New York Times* reported, the electoral vote as well, had the Supreme Court not intervened and stopped the Florida recount.[1]

The *Times* noted, "[A] statewide recount could have produced enough votes to tilt the election [Gore's] way, no matter what standard was chosen to judge voter intent." Unfortunately, they buried that sentence in the 17th paragraph of a story with a misleading headline, because the country had just been attacked on 9/11 and Bush's "legitimacy" was important to preserve during a time of national crisis. And, of course, none of that includes considerations of the considerable voter suppression that then-Governor Jeb Bush and Secretary of State Katherine Harris engaged in, as documented by E.J. Dionne in the *Washington Post*[2] and Greg Palast for the BBC.[3]

More recently, to keep the Court in GOP hands, Senate Majority Leader Mitch McConnell, R-Ky., simply flatly refused to even recognize President Barack Obama's nomination of Merrick Garland to the Supreme Court, waiting for Donald Trump to put in one of the most hard-right justices, Neil Gorsuch, since the 1920s.[4]

The second way around *Citizens United* is for Congress to pass legislation specifically undoing *Citizens United*. Their authority to do this is found in the Constitution, Article 3, Section 2, which says, "[T]he Supreme Court shall have appellate Jurisdiction, both as to Law and Fact, with such Exceptions, and under such Regulations as the Congress shall make." Congress rarely does this (it's referred to as "court stripping"), although banning judicial review was pushed hard in the 1980s, including by Ronald Reagan himself.[5,6]

The third and most likely way to get around this corruption of the Supreme Court is like Congress's ultimate (post–Civil War) response to the Court's *Dred Scott v. Sandford* ruling that African-Americans were property and not people under the Constitution. Congress and the states amended the Constitution (the 13th, 14th, and 15th Amendments) to overturn the Supreme Court's ruling.

Numerous groups, from Public Citizen to Move to Amend, are working hard on this last effort to say, "Corporations are not people and aren't entitled to the rights of personhood" and "Money is not the same thing as speech." If successful, such a constitutional amendment would overturn the "new laws" promulgated (unconstitutionally) by the

Court in 1886 (corporate personhood) and 1976 (money = "free speech").[7,8]

The NRA and their weapons-manufacturing buddies aren't the only bad actors damaging America's body politic through what were once illegal methods to corrupt public officials. Companies from the fossil fuel industry to the GMO industry to Silicon Valley have been doing it for years.

These are all symptoms of the real and larger problem: that the Supreme Court has ruled that corporations and billionaires can own a virtually unlimited number of state and federal politicians. These newly empowered billionaires are now even bragging about that ownership, as Americans can see with the Koch network's announcement that they'd inject an eye-popping $400 million into the 2018 midterms.[9]

Only when America gets money out of politics, as the good citizens of Montana did (temporarily) back in 1912, will the nation be able to deal with the NRA and their ilk on anything like a level playing field.

Neoliberalism Drives Inequality; Inequality Drives Mass Murder

*Among the new objects that attracted my attention during my
stay in the United States, none struck me with greater force
than the equality of conditions. I easily perceived the enormous
influence that this primary fact exercises on the workings of
the society.*

–Alexis de Tocqueville, *Democracy in America* (1835),
**on how economic equality in America strengthens democracy and
reduces violence**

While Ronald Reagan ran for governor of California, his campaign promises to "send the welfare bums back to work" and "clean up the mess at Berkeley" were a thinly veiled code for the fact that he planned to gut the social safety net and suppress dissent. And that's what he did, kicking off a half century of neoliberal austerity economics that have caused inequality in America to skyrocket.

As governor, Reagan deployed armed state police and the National Guard to put down student protests, telling reporters in 1970, "If it takes a bloodbath, let's get it over with. No more appeasement."[1]

As discussed earlier in this book, Reagan signed the Mulford Act into law in reaction to the Black Panthers' arming themselves for protection against racist policing, thereby affirming the racist roots of the Second Amendment.

As a presidential candidate, Reagan dog-whistled to gun-toting southern racists when he declared himself, in his first public speech since being nominated for president, the "law and order" candidate in Philadelphia, Mississippi—in the same county where gun-toting southern racists had brutally tortured and murdered civil rights workers Chaney, Goodman, and Schwerner just 26 years earlier.

And as president, Reagan attacked the American social safety net and pursued economic policies that destroyed the American middle class and drove economic inequality to new heights. As part of his attacks on the social safety net, Reagan also cut funding for federal mental health programs, simply tossing mental health patients out on the street.

Research over the last 25 years shows that there is a close connection between inequality and mental illness, and between inequality and gun violence. Because Reagan gutted federal mental health programs and began the disintegration of the American middle class, his policies have played a large role in creating the current crisis of gun violence and mass shootings.

The Equality Trust is a United Kingdom–based charity that studies the impacts of inequality and "works to improve the quality of life in the UK by reducing economic and social inequality."[2]

According to the Equality Trust, "The link between inequality and homicide rates has been shown in as many as 40 studies, and the differences are large: there are five-fold differences in murder rates between different countries related to inequality. The most important reason why violence is more common in more unequal societies is that it is often triggered by people feeling looked down, disrespected and loss of face."[3]

Mark Kaplan, a professor of social welfare at the UCLA Luskin School of Public Affairs, highlighted this connection between gun violence and inequality in a lecture on January 26, 2017. "You all hear about poverty, but inequality is another measure of economic well-being. And there is a strong correlation between homicide per million and income inequality," Kaplan told students.

Even the Sporting Shooters' Association of Australia has pointed to research out of Belgium showing that "the lower the income per person and the greater the wealth inequality, the higher the expected rate of homicide."[4] That study looked at 52 nonconflict countries with "moderate political regimes," excluding the United States and Australia.[5]

A *Mother Jones* analysis in 2018 found 98 mass shootings in the United States between 1982 and 2018. In 97 of those shootings, the shooter was male. In 56 of those shootings, the shooter was a white male. The average age of the shooter was 35.[6] This means that based on the trend over the last 40 years, the most likely person to commit the next mass shooting in the United States is a relatively young white male.

Mark Follman, Gavin Aronsen, and Deanna Pan at *Mother Jones* add that "a majority were mentally troubled—and many displayed signs of mental health problems before setting out to kill."[7]

It's no coincidence that since 1966, and especially since 1982, we've seen an uptick of young white males taking up arms to shoot civilians in the United States.

It's a matter of social history and economics.

In the 1960s, poor and working-class white Americans, particularly in the South, felt that they were losing something because of the civil rights movement. During this time, the gun was used frequently to preserve the South's racist status quo.

Most notoriously, Martin Luther King Jr. was shot to death as he worked to unite poor whites and poor blacks along class lines. That effort would have disrupted the story about southern hierarchy that had been maintained since the failure of Reconstruction: being a poor white was supposed to be better than being a poor black.

A current example of racism leading to a mass shooting is the case of Dylann Roof, who assassinated a South Carolina state senator and shot eight other people to death after he had scrawled a racist manifesto. He wrote explicitly that he hoped to start a race war.

White men in America also felt like they were losing out to women as a new wave of feminism swept the nation following the 1961 introduction of the first birth control pill and the 1973 legalization of abortion.

Revealing how some American males felt about second-wave feminism, *New York Post* reporter and satirist

Art Buchwald wrote dismissively of a protest against the Miss America pageant. "As we saw in Chicago," Buchwald said, "there are still many men who would like to club women over the head, if they're given the slightest excuse, and there is no better excuse for hitting a woman than the fact that she looks just like a man."[8]

Women in the 1960s had started vying for access to more traditionally "male" jobs, and women started demanding more than just the *Leave It to Beaver* role of stay-at-home wives and homemakers.

This assault on the "old boys' club" left some men feeling emasculated by so-called feminazis as men saw their traditional roles of hunter and breadwinner eroding. Buchwald summed up the misogynist response in his reporting on the Miss America protest: "The protesters think they're bringing about a revolution," Buchwald sneered, "when in fact they're turning back the clock to pre-civilization days when men and women did look and smell alike."

This sense of emasculation continues on today with "men's rights activists" declaring that they need to take back traditional men's roles and push back against perceived discrimination. This type of alienation drove Elliot Rodger, an avowed men's rights activist, to commit the 2014 killings in Isla Vista, California.

White American men felt further alienated as jobless white Americans were competing more and more with black Americans when the American economy suffered massive inflation in the 1970s. Then, in the 1980s, Reagan started the disastrous experiment in Reaganomics, waged war on unions, implemented austerity measures, and declared an explicit war against the social safety net. As a result, the generation that came up during this time was the first generation to experience less social mobility than their parents.

According to a 2015 study published in the *Proceedings of the National Academy of Sciences*, "After the productivity slowdown in the early 1970s, and with widening income inequality, many of the baby-boom generation are the first to find, in midlife, that they will not be better off than were their parents."[9]

Also in 2015, the Congressional Research Service published a report that found that the rate of mass shootings in the United States steadily increased from 1.1 mass public shootings per year in the 1970s to 4.1 shootings per year in the 2000s.[10]

As Eric Levitz pointed out at MSNBC, "The slight increase in mass public shootings in the last four decades is noteworthy, considering that the overall rate of gun crime has declined significantly over the same time period."[11]

In 2017, data scientists Adam R. Pah and Luis Amaral and sociologist John Hagan published research showing that school shootings increase with economic insecurity.

The Northwestern University study looked at the period between 1990 and 2013. According to Hagan, it found that "the link between education and work is central to our expectations about economic opportunity and upward mobility in America. Our study indicates that increases in gun violence in our schools can result from disappointment and despair during periods of increased unemployment, when getting an education does not necessarily lead to finding work."[12]

Based on the evidence, there is a clear connection between inequality, gun violence, and mass shootings. The last 38 years of failed neoliberal economics, combined with social changes over the last century, have left white men in America feeling disadvantaged and desperate.

Because they feel disempowered and emasculated, they pick up a gun to try to exercise control by lashing out at society in the most direct and most potent way: indiscriminate killing.

Reagan's economic policies marked the beginning of the neoliberal experiment, which weakened the middle class and caused inequality to skyrocket in America. And no president since Reagan has ever seriously addressed the fundamental economic and social issues that are driving inequality and social despair—which in turn are driving America's culture of gun violence and mass shootings.

Addressing mass shootings in America requires also addressing the economic and social conditions that help create mass shooters.

CHAPTER 25

Weapons of War on America's Streets

Yes, people pull the trigger—but guns are the instrument of death. Gun control is necessary, and delay means more death and horror.

–Former New York governor Eliot Spitzer

America has a deep and complex problem with guns, which simultaneously draws on the history of genocide and slavery, the ongoing and widespread hatred and/or fear of people of color by a significant portion of America's white population, and the interconnection of "conservative" media like Fox and right-wing talk radio.

There are multiple strategies to dial back gun violence, most drawing on the experience of other nations. The key to all of them is to reduce the overall number of guns in circulation; numerous studies show that there is a clear and simple association between the number of guns in circulation and the frequency and severity of gun violence.

As David Hemenway, director of the Harvard Injury Control Center, told the *New York Times'* Elisabeth Rosenthal, "Generally, if you live in a civilized society, more guns means more death. There is no evidence that having more guns reduces crime. None at all."[1]

Similarly, when the new mayor of Bogotá, Colombia, banned carrying guns in cars or in public in 2010, the homicide rate in the city dropped by 50 percent.[2]

Given both the anecdotal evidence of the radical drop in deaths and crime in country after country that make it harder to buy and own guns, and the multiple scientific studies that back up that observation, it appears that two simple changes to US law—both based in other laws that Americans already know well and like, could solve most of America's gun-violence problem. They are:

1. Treat all semiautomatic weapons in a similar way under the same laws as fully automatic weapons.

2. Regulate gun ownership and usage the same way America regulates car ownership and usage.

CHAPTER 26

Semiautomatic Weapons

Semi-automatics have only two purposes. One is so owners can take them to the shooting range once in awhile, yell yeehaw, and get all horny at the rapid fire and the burning vapor spurting from the end of the barrel. Their other use—their only other use—is to kill people.

–Stephen King, *Guns*

Back in the Prohibition era, before and during the time John Dillinger and friends were shooting up American cities from New York to Chicago to San Francisco, the National Rifle Association approved of two very consequential laws that restricted gun ownership and use.

(The NRA didn't become a lobbying and promotional front group for the weapons industry until the 1970s, when the Supreme Court's *Buckley v. Valeo* and *First National Bank of Boston v. Bellotti* decisions ruled that wealthy gun-manufacturing corporations could legally buy and own their very own politicians. For nearly a century prior to that, the NRA supported rational gun control.)

The Uniform Firearms Act of 1931 in Pennsylvania was the harbinger of the federal National Firearms Act of 1934, which brought an end to the widespread legal availability of fully automatic "tommy guns," along with, later, silencers and sawed-off shotguns. But ownership of such automatic weapons isn't really banned—it's just a somewhat complex process to get permission to own and use them.

First, the applicant must find a local law enforcement officer who will vouch for him or her and perform a background check. His or her signature is the necessary first step to getting a permit to own an automatic weapon,[1] and the applicant must have an absolutely clean record, from a clean criminal record to not owing any child support to not having any past firearms violations. If someone lies about this, or applies for a permit through a "clean" third party, they and their third party could both end up in jail.

Then the applicant must pull together two sets of fingerprints and two passport-type photos, plus the $200 "tax stamp" fee for the permit, and get all the information on the gun, including its serial number and details on its last owner.

Finally, he or she needs to fill out an "OMB No. 1140-0014 Application for Tax Paid Transfer and Registration of Firearm" form, with such easy questions as category 14:

1. Are you under indictment or information in any court for a felony, or any other crime, for which the judge could imprison you for more than one year?

2. Have you ever been convicted in any court for a felony, or any other crime, for which the judge could have imprisoned you for more than one year, even if you received a shorter sentence including probation? *(See definition 1m.)*

3. Are you a fugitive from justice?

4. Are you an unlawful user of, or addicted to, marijuana or any depressant, stimulant, narcotic drug, or any other controlled substance?

5. Have you ever been adjudicated as a mental defective OR have you ever been committed to a mental institution?

6. Have you been discharged from the Armed Forces under dishonorable conditions?

7. Are you subject to a court order restraining you from harassing, stalking, or threatening your child or an intimate partner or child of such partner?

8. Have you ever been convicted in any court of a misdemeanor crime of domestic violence?

Applicants also have to provide the government with the reason why they think it appropriate for them to have a fully automatic weapon, sawed-off shotgun, or other "destructive device":

13. Transferee Necessity Statement:

I _____ have a reasonable necessity to possess the machinegun, short-barreled rifle, short-barreled shotgun, or destructive device described on this application for the following reason(s) _____ _____ and my possession of the device or weapon would be consistent with public safety (18 U.S.C. § 922(b)(4) and 27 CFR § 478.98).

Karl Frederick, the NRA's president back when these laws were put into place, was enthusiastic. "I have never believed in the general practice of carrying weapons," he said. "I think it should be sharply restricted and only under licenses."

When Frederick was asked if he thought the National Firearms Act of 1934 violated a person's Second Amendment rights, he famously said, "I have not given it any study from that point of view."

The result of the restrictions on ownership of fully automatic weapons (and other "destructive devices") has been that they've pretty much vanished as the scourge on public safety that they were in the late 1920s and early 1930s.

Thus, it's rare that either fully automatic weapons or the less-efficient-at-killing-lots-of-people revolvers and bolt-action rifles are used for mass murders. This is largely because the former are hard to buy/own; and for the latter, the time necessary to re-cock and reload presents victims an opportunity to stop a mass shooting.

Remember, the only reason why the shooter who tried to kill Rep. Gabrielle Giffords in Tucson, Arizona, was stopped after "only" killing six people was that he had to replace his 33-shot magazine with a fresh one, and Bill Badger, a 74-year-old man standing near him (whom he'd just shot), tackled him and held him to the ground.[2]

Thus, as the volume of production of semiautomatic weapons has increased in the past 30 years or so, and their price has come down, the older-fashioned pistols and bolt-action rifles have been replaced by a more recent generation of semiautomatic pistols, rifles, and assault weapons.

But if most handguns in circulation were revolvers, and most rifles were bolt- or break-action, there would be far fewer (or at least far less deadly) mass shootings.

Revolvers typically have a cylinder that holds five to 10 rounds of ammunition, and each chamber in the cylinder must be individually loaded. While there are autoloaders and other ways to speed up the process, the gun is still largely limited, at least in an "active shooter" situation, to the rounds in its cylinder.

With a revolver, the gun can't even be fired until it's cocked by pulling back the hammer or pulling hard enough on the trigger to cock the hammer.

Revolvers are very efficient killing machines, having been in widespread use since their popularization by the Colt Company in the 1830s, but while they're great for sport and self-defense (and were police weapons of choice until the past 30 or so years), for mass killings they can't hold a candle to semiautomatics.

Semiautomatic pistols are, in their modern form, a creation of the last century. They use the recoil force of a shot (some also use the exhaust gases) to load a new round into the chamber and cock the gun, all in one seamless and nearly instantaneous motion.

As a result, semiautomatics can be fired as fast as one can pull the trigger, and the amount of trigger pressure that a revolver would require to cock the hammer is unnecessary. And because they don't have a built-in cylinder like a revolver, the magazine in a semiautomatic that stores the ammunition (some as large as 50 shots) can be quickly replaced.

The rifle side of the equation is largely the same: while bolt-action rifles don't have a cylinder, they do require the shooter to pull back the bolt between shots, which ejects the spent shell, inserts a new one, and re-cocks the weapon itself. Variations on this include lever-action and pump-action rifles or shotguns, although all require action by the shooter between shots.

Semiautomatic rifles, on the other hand, like semiautomatic pistols, use recoil or gases to reload and re-cock the weapon, so that shots can be squeezed off as fast as the shooter can pull the trigger. And because—like semiautomatic pistols—they have quickly replaceable magazines, they're far deadlier than bolt-pump or break-action rifles.

Since the vast majority of mass murders of the 1930s were accomplished with fully automatic weapons, tightly regulating who could buy and own them pretty much removed mass murders from the streets of America. It's time to do the same with semiautomatic weapons, which are the new mass killers' weapons of choice.

All it would take would be amending the National Firearms Act to put any semiautomatic gun of any kind under the same sort of oversight and permitting necessary for fully automatic weapons.

CHAPTER 27

What America Learned from Cars—and How to Apply It to Guns

A lot of the people who keep a gun at home for safety are the same ones who refuse to wear a seat belt.

–George Carlin

While there were a number of automobile manufacturing companies in the late 19th century, it was really at the turn of the 20th century that cars became a hot commodity in the United States.

R. E. Olds rolled out the first assembly line in 1901, but it was Henry Ford who cranked the popularity of cars up a notch with his "first version" of the Model A in 1903, and then developed the assembly line to crank out the Model T in 1908.

By 1927, around the time he rolled out the "second version" of his Model A, he'd sold more than 15 million cars.

So it was that, around 1915, many states began to notice that cars were killing people. They were being hit on the roads, dying when drivers didn't know how to avoid running into trees or off bridges, and having accidents with horse-drawn carts and other automobiles.

This presented the lawmakers of most states with a serious question: what to do to protect the public, including the car owners, from the dangers of death and disfigurement that cars presented?

The answer that most states came up with, and has now largely been standardized across the US and most of the world, was a very simple and straightforward three-part criterion for car ownership and operation.

1. **Establish ownership.** In order to be able to manage all the cars coming onto the roads, both as valuable pieces of theft-worthy hardware and to track liability issues, all cars were required to have a Vehicle Identification Number (VIN), which was stamped onto the car during manufacture and followed it until the day it was destroyed or decommissioned. Similarly, the owner of that car and its VIN had to present himself or herself to state authorities and sign a title of ownership, which had to be recorded with the state whenever the title was transferred to a new owner.

2. **Prove competence.** By the years around 1915 there had been so many fatalities and serious injuries attributable to cars that the states decided they wanted only people driving on public roads who knew how to handle a car properly. This meant defining rules for the road, having people learn those rules, and testing them—both in writing and practically in person—to show that they truly could drive safely. When people passed the tests, they were given a license to drive.

3. **Require liability insurance.** Because virtually all car accidents were just that—accidents— most people who "caused" accidents were at both financial and legal risk. Many were fine, upstanding citizens (in fact, because cars were expensive, most car owners fell into this broad category). And they wanted some defense against the chance of making a mistake and ending up in jail or broke because of lawsuits or the liability costs of caring for people they'd injured. What came out of this was the development of automobile liability insurance and the establishment of a requirement for it to be carried by all owners/drivers. While most states adopted this requirement substantially later than 1915, it's now established as a fundamental part of the three steps necessary to drive a car.

Which brings us to today.

These three things that America does for owners of cars are perfect to deal with America's gun problem:

- Registration and title—as a requirement rather than an option—would establish a clear chain of custody and responsibility, so that when people behaved irresponsibly with their guns, they could be held to account.

- Having a shooter's license be conditional on passing both a written and a shooting-range test would demonstrate competence and also insert a trained person into the process who could spot "off kil-ter" people like the Parkland shooter. Taking a cue from most other countries, America could also require people to prove a need or sporting/safety use for a weapon.

• Today, if a car had run down mass-shooting vic-tims, their families would be getting millions from GEICO, et al. Because a gun killed them, they get nothing. This is bizarre in the extreme; all Ameri-cans end up paying the costs of gun violence. The simple solution is to require all gun owners to carry liability insurance, just like all drivers must. The insurance would even be a "free market" solu-tion in that, as with cars, insurers would charge much more (or even refuse coverage) to "high risk" people, such as those with domestic assault convictions.

These three steps are nothing but common sense and don't infringe on the "rights" of gun owners any more than they infringe on the "rights" of car owners. They could even provide a stream of revenue for gun-owners' organizations that chose to train people to prepare for their licensure test and/or offer low-cost liability insurance.

CHAPTER 28

Gun Manufacturing in the 21st Century: 3-D Printing

The future masters of technology will have to be light-hearted and intelligent. The machine easily masters the grim and the dumb.

–Marshall McLuhan

In August 2018, a district court judge in Seattle effectively banned the free sharing of 3-D printed gun blueprints on the internet. Cody Wilson, the founder of an open-source gun company called Defense Distributed, responded with an announcement that he would sell the blueprints to people who wanted them. After all, the injunction simply said that Wilson couldn't *freely distribute* his blueprints; but he is absolutely allowed to sell the blueprints, at least to United States citizens. If he sells to someone who is not a US citizen, he will violate US export laws.[1]

As with any new technology, people are concerned about the consequences. People are concerned that any average American will be able to manufacture his or her own gun, and that 3-D printed guns essentially make any gun regulations or background checks worthless.

But self-manufacturing something doesn't place it beyond the law. For instance, despite the panic over freely available gun-printing blueprints, there are already two basic regulations in place: Wilson can't give away his blueprints, and he can't sell blueprints to non-US citizens.

And beyond those very basic regulations, there are already plenty of models for regulating homemade products: everything from cars to raw milk to homemade liquor is regulated in the United States, even if it is manufactured or produced at home.

For example, the laws surrounding homemade cars in Oregon provide a blueprint for regulating 3-D printed guns. In Oregon there are five basic requirements for certifying an "assembled, reconstructed or replica vehicle" so that someone can drive it on public roads:[2]

A. Title or Salvage Title for the frame or unibody used in the vehicle (if not previously surrendered to DMV).

B. Evidence of ownership for each major part used, such as bill(s) of sale, a title or a Manufacturer's Certificate of Origin (MCO). If building or rebuilding a vehicle from a kit, you must provide the MCO for the kit. Major parts may be the body (if not unibody), engine, kit, or axles (if a trailer).

C. Application for Title and Registration (Form 735-226). The vehicle description in Section 1 must match the application.

D. Applicable fees.

E. Vehicle Identification Number (VIN) inspection.

And that's not all! Remember that all car owners must also have car insurance, and they must possess a state-issued driver's license. How a car is manufactured does not change any of these requirements.

Under a common-sense set of gun regulations, 3-D printed guns should be required to be registered and the owner licensed to carry, just like with automobiles. And just like with a homemade automobile, if someone were caught in possession of an unregistered 3-D printed gun, then he or she would face fines or jail time.

CHAPTER **29** ///

Well-Regulated
Smart Guns Are Here

*The biggest enemy of western people is not war or terrorism,
it is their own governments' lack of regulation of
public health and safety.*
–British author and engineer Steven Magee

In the United States (as with every other developed country
in the world), we regulate a wide variety of consumer goods.
Children's toys must be safe, designed in ways that they don't
present a choking risk and don't contain paint or ingredients
that are toxic or cancer-causing. Our furniture and carpets have
to meet minimum fire standards. Cars, because they're capable
of killing people, are heavily regulated to be safer in collisions
and designed with sight lines that make collisions less likely.

From the development of seat belts and airbags in cars
to lawsuits that highlight safety dangers with toys and push
manufacturers to improve things, virtually every time dangers
are identified or new "safety" technologies become available,
they're applied to products manufactured and/or sold in
America.

Except guns.

A company named Safe Gun Technology, Inc., for example, developed a fingerprint reader that's built right into the

140

grip on handguns and rifles, preventing the weapon from being fired by anybody except those people "authorized" to shoot it by having their fingerprints in its system.[1] Their fingerprint reader, simply a flat spot on the grip where a fingertip would normally lay, can even be retrofitted onto existing weapons.

Another company, Intelligun, offers a similar finger-print-reading product and is working with the US Army's Armament Research, Development and Engineering Center to come up with a stock that, instead of recognizing finger-prints (which can be obscured by dirt, etc.), measures exactly how and where the authorized user grips his or her gun, another biometric measure that's highly personalized.

Radio frequency identification (RFID) recognition of a gun's owner, thus unlocking the weapon, has become a mature industry; TriggerSmart Technologies sells a gun that unlocks when handled by a user who's wearing a ring that the gun recognizes. The German company Armatix sells a gun that unlocks by RFID with a watch worn by the owner.

Microstamping is a technology whereby the firing pin has a tiny serial number etched into it, which transfers to the bul-let when it's struck by the pin, leaving a dent with the number on it. This allows law enforcement to instantly identify the gun from which the bullet was fired and, if it's registered, instantly identify the owner as well. California passed a law in 2007 to mandate this and was immediately sued; however, the law withstood judicial review.

But none of these technologies are making any significant inroads in the American gun market. In fact, gun dealers who've tried to sell these products have been threatened, including explicit death threats.

Fortune magazine reported on a man named "Doug" who started and ran a website, now closed, at smartgunz.com, that promoted safer guns and offered the Armatix (RFID with a watch) gun for sale. He wouldn't give his last name to *Fortune*, though, because he feared for his life.

As Roger Parloff wrote in *Fortune*, "And that's why Doug has to be so hush-hush. If his last name were made public, people would try to put him out of business and, perhaps, threaten to kill him. That's what happened to the last two gun dealers who tried to sell this gun."[2]

It's as if the car industry had succeeded in their 1970s campaign against having to put seat belts and airbags into cars, and thus instead of only around 35,000 people a year dying in car crashes, the number was two or three times that. And car enthusiasts or agents of the auto industry were threatening the lives of people offering to sell aftermarket seat belts or running websites advocating for them.

Senator Elizabeth Warren, D-Mass., introduced legislation requiring one of these sorts of safety devices to be built into any new guns sold in America; Republican leadership in the Senate refused to even consider it in committee, much less bring it to the floor for a vote.

"Gun violence has become far too common in America," Warren said when introducing another law that would close the gun-show loophole. "Thoughts and prayers just aren't enough. Congress has a moral responsibility to take common sense actions to stop this epidemic.... [I]t's time to take these weapons of war off of our streets. And we need to do more to fix our broken background check system, to keep guns away from felons and other dangerous people."[3]

It's time to regulate guns in the United States. Variations on the word "regulate" appear eight times in the body of the Constitution and, ironically, in the Second Amendment. There's no practical or legal impediment to regulating guns to make them safer—except the lobbying power of the gun industry and the few gun owners who behave like cultists.

Addressing Racism to Reduce Gun Violence

He got his fat dreams, he got his slaves
He got his profits, he owns our cage,
He has his prisons, he has his gates
He has his judges, they have our fate.
–Richie Havens, "Fates"

Louise Hartmann was lucky, for a white girl. When she was 14 or so, the public high school she attended in East Lansing, Michigan, had a mandatory school-wide "Black Awareness" class.

She read everything from Alan Paton's 1948 classic novel about South Africa, *Cry, the Beloved Country*, to the writings of Malcolm X and Martin Luther King Jr. She learned the history of slavery, Reconstruction, Jim Crow, *Brown v. Board of Education*, and the civil rights laws being passed those very years she was in school, and came to understand what redlining and other forms of institutional racism meant.

"It changed my life, even before I became an adult," my wife recalls. "That experience altered forever how I understand race in America and gave me a deep empathy for the challenges people of color face in my nation—and around the world."

The simple fact of the matter is that, as noted repeatedly in this book, genocide and racism are interpenetrated with and driven by racist laws, policies, and racial theories that purely benefit Caucasians and have turned America into a hyper-armed camp with more guns than people. And, as noted in the story in the introduction, white racism continues to animate the gun issue in this country daily, in ways large and small.

For white Americans older than 30 who've had little contact with black, Hispanic, Asian, or native people, their understanding of such folk is deeply rooted in racist stereotypes. From cartoons and movies to TV shows, from the 1930s to the 1980s, pretty much every depiction of a minority was as either a villain or a buffoon.

We've come a long way from Buckwheat, Jemima, and even *Sanford and Son*. Young white people today are far more likely to understand race in a holistic way and to have friends or acquaintances who differ from them racially. But there's still a long way to go to achieving both racial equality and racial reconciliation in this nation.

Integration is proven to be one of the most effective ways to diminish the racially charged impulses that drive everything from killer cops to vigilantes like George Zimmerman to white nationalists like Dylann Roof. Once a person has had the real-life experience of getting to know "the other," that otherness generally dissipates rapidly. To this goal, the racial "forced busing" of the 1960s was a positive first step; a national conversation is needed to determine what would be the next few steps to bringing people together.

Similarly, reparations in the form of affirmative action programs have lifted many poor people of color into quality

jobs and educational opportunities, helping to create a substantial black and Hispanic middle class.

Perhaps the biggest barrier to equality of opportunities
among the races is our public school system. Unlike pretty
much anywhere else in the world, we pay for local public
schools with local property taxes.

The consequence—the intended effect, in fact—is that
poor and minority schools lack the resources needed for a
quality education and turn out students who can't effectively
compete in the modern world. Wealthy neighborhoods, on
the other hand, turn out students with well-rounded educa-
tions who can easily make the transition into quality colleges
and then into high-paying jobs.

Thus, when poor black kids from poor neighborhoods
can't perform to reading or math or science standards, the
white racists say, essentially, "See, I told you they're inferior.
And, because they're not so bright and are poor, I definitely
need a gun to protect myself from them."

This one issue—property-tax-funded schools—is one of
the greatest drivers of intergenerational poverty. It's urgent
that state, county, and city legislative bodies reject this system nationwide and move to fully funded and high-quality
standardized education in every community in America.
And that requires elimination of local funding of schools;
they should be funded statewide and required to perform to
national standards.

The other institution in America deeply in need of reform
is our system of policing and imprisonment.

Inroads are being made, although they're mostly in more affluent or well-funded communities, in part because, again, local property taxes pay a portion of local policing. There are also no national standards for hiring, training, and supervising police.

Washington, DC, has lately integrated racial awareness classes into the curriculum for officers; it's a single, all-day class that includes a visit to the new National Museum of African American History and Culture. One of the teachers noted to the *Washingtonian* magazine that "at the end of one session, a white, 25-year veteran of the force asked, with tears in his eyes, if he was a racist because he treated people in [black area] Shaw and [wealthy white] Georgetown differently. After another class, an officer came up to Thompson and put it more simply: 'I didn't know. I didn't know.'"[1] More police departments must make this small start, at the very least.

Meanwhile, the private prison industry is one of the fastest-growing industries in the United States as of this writing, and their lobbyists and campaign contributions are generally directed not toward high standards for rehabilitation, as in other developed nations, but instead toward longer sentences for more types of crimes.

In both education and imprisonment, the profit motive has been highly corrosive of equal justice under the law, particularly when comparing communities that are racially different. Private prisons should be banned, as they are in most other developed countries, and public schools and police departments need national funding and national standards.

CHAPTER **31**

Learning from
Other Nations

*The results are clear. Gun deaths are a problem amenable to
reduction like any other public health problem.
International differences in rates between countries show this.
The United States has the worst record of gun deaths of any
[developed] nation, exceeded only by that in chaotic nations with
massive law and order problems.*
**–Simon Chapman, professor at the University of Sydney's School of
Public Health and lead author of a peer-reviewed study on the impact of
Australia's 1996 gun-control laws**

Just as most Americans have no idea that every other developed country in the world has already figured out how to inex-
pensively and efficiently provide health care for 100 percent
of its citizens as a right, so, too, most Americans have no idea
how all the other developed nations of the world have man-
aged to keep their gun-deaths-per-hundred-thousand-people
rate below 0.5, while in the United States it's more than 6 people killed with guns per 100,000 citizens.

But other countries have done it, and America can learn a
lot from their experience.

This is largely the path that Australia has taken.

After a decades-long series of mass shootings, culmi-
nating in the 1996 Port Arthur Massacre, that nation, in a
moment of collective revulsion, chose to require a license to

148

own virtually any type of gun and to regulate semiautomatic pistols and rifles as tightly as fully automatic ones.

They also put into place a series of national amnesty and gun-buyback programs, which pulled hundreds of thousands of now-illegal guns out of circulation in that country, while appropriately compensating former gun owners.

It's still relatively easy for hunters and sportsmen and women to get pistols or rifles. All they have to do is prove that they are who they say they are, pass a background test, and then prove on an ongoing basis that they're actually using their weapons for sport, at least annually.

Since the implementation of these laws in 1996, Australia has had only one mass shooting incident, and that was relatively small. In the first years after the laws took place, firearm-related deaths in Australia fell by well over 40 percent, with suicides dropping by 77 percent.

And it's not just Australia.

Every other developed or developing country in the world has more stringent gun-control laws than the United States.[1] Which may be why no other such country has the horrific rate of gun deaths and mass shootings that Americans experience daily.

None of these solutions are difficult.

We've done them all before in other areas (like car ownership and fully automatic weapons) and they've worked fine, and every other developed country in the world has successfully applied them to guns.

America can, too.

The NRA and industry front groups are losing their power daily, and American politicians are increasingly gathering the courage to stop taking the NRA's money. Thankfully, folks like the young people of Parkland, Florida, and victims groups from previous mass shootings are doing everything they can to make that happen. They deserve America's support.

A clear-eyed understanding of America's past, and a broad knowledge of how a gun-industry-driven effort to rewrite America's laws and distort this nation's history has increased their profits while killing hundreds of thousands of Americans, is necessary to begin the work of unwinding the spiraling gun violence in America. The price this country has paid, a growing national consensus says, is too high.

As Americans awaken to the very real possibility of living in a country that's not torn apart by gunfire, this nation can work together to save lives while simultaneously increasing everybody's access to *life, liberty, and the pursuit of happiness.*

NOTES

Preface

1. His actual words were much more obscene; I've cleaned this up for a family-friendly book.
2. Ibid.
3. Ibid.
4. https://en.wikipedia.org/wiki/2008–13_United_States_ammunition_shortage
5. https://www.nytimes.com/2012/12/16/nyregion/friends-of-gunmans-mother-his-first-victim-recall-her-as-generous.html
6. http://www.pewsocialtrends.org/2013/05/07/gun-homicide-rate-down-49-since-1993-peak-public-unaware/
7. https://en.wikipedia.org/wiki/List_of_countries_by_firearm-related_death_rate
8. https://everytownresearch.org/gun-violence-america/

Introduction

1. Marianne Williamson, "Marianne Williamson's Plea to Sarah Palin: Words Have Power," *HuffPost*, June 1, 2010, https://www.huffingtonpost.com/marianne-williamson/marianne-williamsons-plea_b_520888.html.
2. https://theconversation.com/quantifying-the-social-cost-of-firearms-a-new-approach-to-gun-control-62148
3. https://injuryprevention.bmj.com/content/12/6/365.full
4. https://www.independent.co.uk/news/world/americas/us-gun-deaths-killings-control-homicides-america-shootings-a8285916.html
5. Ibid.
6. Ibid.
7. https://theconversation.com/quantifying-the-social-cost-of-firearms-a-new-approach-to-gun-control-62148
8. Derived by dividing $300 billion by the 2017 statistic of 126 million households.
9. https://thinkprogress.org/study-gun-violence-hospitalizations-cost-over-600-million-in-2010-alone-c36561775030/
10. https://www.theatlantic.com/health/archive/2018/02/gun-violence-public-health/553430/

11. https://www.washingtonpost.com/opinions/we-wont-know-the-cause-of-gun-violence-until-we-look-for-it/2012/07/27/gJQAPfenEX_story.html
12. http://abcnews.go.com/US/federal-government-study-gun-violence/story?id=50300379
13. http://pediatrics.aappublications.org/content/140/1/e20163486
14. https://www.washingtonpost.com/news/wonk/wp/2017/06/20/19-children-are-shot-every-day-in-the-united-states/?utm_term=.40c2cc7de6b8
15. https://www.nytimes.com/2013/09/29/us/children-and-guns-the-hidden-toll.html

Chapter 1

1. US Works Projects Administration, *Slave Narratives: A Folk History of Slavery in the United States, from Interviews with Former Slaves—Tennessee Narratives* (Fili-Quarian Classics, 2010).
2. https://www.nytimes.com/2017/11/07/world/americas/mass-shootings-us-international.html
3. https://www.eurekalert.org/pub_releases/2018-11/aaop-ham102218.php
4. https://www.washingtonpost.com/news/wonk/wp/2018/06/19/there-are-more-guns-than-people-in-the-united-states-according-to-a-new-study-of-global-firearm-ownership/?utm_term=.b5931fd07229

Chapter 2

1. Roxanne Dunbar-Ortiz, *Loaded: A Disarming History of the Second Amendment* (San Francisco: City Lights Books), 65–66.
2. https://www.washingtonpost.com/news/post-politics/wp/2014/04/24/cliven-bundy-on-blacks-are-they-better-off-as-slaves/?utm_term=.a25b9da81883
3. https://www.latimes.com/politics/washington/la-na-pol-essential-washington-updates-roy-moore-america-was-great-when-1512758057-htmlstory.html
4. https://www.economist.com/node/218080

Chapter 3

1. https://founders.archives.gov/documents/Washington/03-20-02-0661
2. David E. Stannard, *American Holocaust: The Conquest of the New World*, reprint ed. (New York: Oxford University Press, 1993).

3. https://www.amazon.com/Last-Hours-Ancient-Sunlight-Revised/dp/1400051576/ref=thomhartmann
4. https://www.npr.org/2013/04/06/176132730/the-first-gun-in-america

Chapter 4

1. Jack D. Forbes, *Columbus and Other Cannibals: The Wetiko Disease of Exploitation, Imperialism, and Terrorism*, rev. ed. (New York: Seven Stories Press, 2008).
2. Ibid.
3. Ibid.

Chapter 5

1. Stannard, *American Holocaust.*
2. Tzvetan Todorov, *Memory as a Remedy for Evil* (Chicago: Seagull Books, 2010).
3. This story was first published in 1879 in the *New York Tribune* by "Major Anthony" and is quoted in numerous sources, including its own Wikipedia page on the "Sand Creek Massacre."
4. Jack D. Forbes, *Columbus and Other Cannibals: The Wetiko Disease of Exploitation, Imperialism, and Terrorism* (New York: Seven Stories Press, 2008).
5. Howard Zinn, *A People's History of the United States* (New York: HarperCollins, 2003), 12.

Chapter 6

1. Zinn, *A People's History of the United States*, 12.
2. Ibid.
3. Dunbar-Ortiz, *Loaded*, 65–66.

Chapter 7

1. https://www.washingtonpost.com/news/volokh-conspiracy/wp/2017/11/21/the-american-indian-foundation-of-american-gun-culture/?utm_term=.d901b901fd40
2. Edmund S. Morgan, *American Slavery, American Freedom* (London: W. W. Norton & Co., 1975).
3. https://founders.archives.gov/documents/Jefferson/03-10-02-0158-0002

Chapter 8

1. https://lawreview.law.ucdavis.edu/issues/31/2/Articles/Davis Vol31No2_Bogus.pdf
2. Sally E. Hadden, *Slave Patrols: Law and Violence in Virginia and the Carolinas* (Cambridge, MA: Harvard University Press, 2001).
3. The echoes here of Trayvon Martin's killing by George Zimmerman, walking "neighborhood patrol," are eerie.

Chapter 10

1. Federal Writers' Project: Slave Narrative Project, Vol. 11, North Carolina, Part 2, Jackson-Yellerday, https://www.loc.gov/resource/mesn.112/?sp=120.

Chapter 12

1. Jonathan Elliot, ed., *The Debates in the Several State Conventions on the Adoption of the Federal Constitution as Recommended by the General Convention at Philadelphia in 1787*, 5 vols., 2nd ed., 1888, reprint ed. (New York: Burt Franklin, n.d.).

Chapter 13

1. https://www.huffingtonpost.com/adam-winkler/did-the-wild-west-have-mo_b_956035.html
2. https://www.theguardian.com/science/2016/aug/10/black-patients-bias-prescriptions-pain-management-medicine-opioids
3. Jefferson to Chastellux, June 7, 1785: "I beleive [sic] the Indian then to be in body and mind equal to the whiteman . . ."
4. Herbert Spencer, *The Principles of Biology* (London: Williams and Norgate, 1864).
5. http://www.emersonkent.com/speeches/lincoln_dinner_address.htm
6. Hermann Hagedorn, *Roosevelt in the Badlands, Vol. 1* (New York: Houghton Mifflin Co., 1930), 355.
7. "Theodore Roosevelt's 1902 letter on 'race suicide' to Marie Van Horst," https://progressingamerica.blogspot.com/2013/06/theodore-roosevelts-1902-letter-on-race.html.

Chapter 14

1. Quoted in Roy P. Basler, ed., *The Collected Works of Abraham Lincoln, Vol. 4* (New Brunswick, NJ: Rutgers University Press, 1953), 204.
2. https://www.history.com/topics/american-civil-war/john-wilkes-booth

Chapter 15

1. https://www.nps.gov/anjo/learn/historyculture/slaves.htm
2. Hadden, *Slave Patrols*, 194.
3. Ibid., 195.
4. https://newrepublic.com/article/112322/gun-control-racist
5. Hadden, *Slave Patrols*, 202.
6. https://newrepublic.com/article/112322/gun-control-racist

Chapter 16

1. https://www.cnn.com/2016/11/07/politics/can-you-bring-your-gun-to-vote/index.html
2. https://www.battlefields.org/learn/primary-sources/declaration-causes-seceding-states
3. Ibid.
4. http://www.baltimoresun.com/news/maryland/crime/bs-md-ci-gun-trace-task-force-gttf-testimony-highlights-20180126-story.html
5. http://www.cleveland.com/court-justice/index.ssf/2017/01/tamir_rice_shooting_a_breakdow.html
6. https://www.nytimes.com/2018/03/28/us/sacramento-stephon-clark.html

Chapter 17

1. Bobby Seale, *Seize the Time: The Story of the Black Panther Party and Huey P. Newton*, reprint ed. (Baltimore, MD: Black Classic Press, 1996).
2. This story is also told by Adam Winkler in his book *Gunfight: The Battle Over the Right to Bear Arms in America* (New York: W. W. Norton & Co., 2013).
3. http://clerk.assembly.ca.gov/sites/clerk.assembly.ca.gov/files/archive/FinalHistory/1967/Volumes/67ahr.PDF
4. Winkler, *Gunfight*.
5. https://www.washingtonpost.com/news/post-nation/wp/2018/01/08/judge-dismisses-federal-charges-against-nevada-rancher-cliven-bundy-who-calls-himself-a-political-prisoner/
6. https://www.twincities.com/2016/07/07/questions-raised-previously-about-st-anthony-police-encounters-with-permit-to-carry-holders/
7. https://www.washingtonpost.com/national/nra-criticized-for-response-to-police-shooting-of-man-who-allegedly-said-he-had-carry-permit/2016/07/12/0174b698-4770-11e6-bdb9-701687974517_story.html?utm_term=.5bb44b84f110

Chapter 18

1. https://www.texasmonthly.com/articles/96-minutes/
2. https://www.texasmonthly.com/articles/the-madman-on-the-tower/
3. https://www.amazon.com/Mass-Murderers-Crime-Time-Life-Books/dp/0783500041
4. Ibid.
5. http://www.dailytexanonline.com/2016/07/30/experts-still-disagree-on-role-of-tower-shooters-brain-tumor

Chapter 19

1. https://www.washingtonpost.com/news/retropolis/wp/2017/10/02/from-the-ut-tower-to-a-las-vegas-hotel-the-carnage-when-shooters-take-aim-from-above/?noredirect=on&utm_term=.ac4aa0921a72
2. https://www.thelily.com/1077-people-have-been-killed-in-mass-shootings-since-a-1966-incident-at-the-university-of-texas/
3. https://www.berkeley.edu/news/media/releases/2004/06/08_reagan.shtml
4. https://www.oregonlive.com/expo/news/erry-2018/10/7d2bb561246607/what-we-know-about-patriot-pra.html
5. http://time.com/4256809/donald-trump-l/
6. https://www.nytimes.com/2016/08/10/us/politics/donald-trump-hillary-clinton.html
7. https://www.cnn.com/2018/10/28/us/pittsburgh-synagogue-shooting/index.html
8. https://www.cnn.com/2018/11/01/us/irvine-california-synagogue-graffiti-trnd/index.html
9. https://www.nytimes.com/2018/11/02/nyregion/broad-city-jewish-synagogue-anti-semitism.html
10. https://www.nytimes.com/2018/11/03/us/yoga-studio-shooting-florida.html
11. https://www.csis.org/analysis/rise-far-right-extremism-united-states
12. Ibid.
13. https://www.usatoday.com/story/news/nation/2018/11/08/thousand-oaks-california-bar-shooting-307th-mass-shooting/1928574002/

Chapter 20

1. https://www.washingtonpost.com/news/the-watch/wp/2016/01/11/why-the-wet-tea-leaves-drug-raid-was-outrageous/?utm_term=.a6f198ec5a35

2. https://harpers.org/archive/2016/04/legalize-it-all/
3. http://www.thenation.com/article/exclusive-lee-atwaters-infamous-1981-interview-southern-strategy/
4. https://www.huffingtonpost.com/amanda-reiman/marijuana-prohibition-anniversary_b_1923370.html
5. http://www.justicepolicy.org/images/upload/08_01_REP_DrugTx_AC-PS.pdf
6. http://www.naacp.org/pages/criminal-justice-fact-sheet
7. http://www.drugpolicy.org/wasted-tax-dollars

Chapter 21

1. https://www.supremecourt.gov/opinions/07pdf/07-290.pdf
2. "James Madison's Notes from the 1787 Philadelphia Convention," http://www.nhccs.org/Mnotes.html.
3. US House of Representatives debate on the Bill of Rights, June 1789, http://press-pubs.uchicago.edu/founders/documents/bill_of_rightss11.html.
4. Bob Drogin, "Gun Control Was Tougher in Old Tombstone," *Washington Post*, February 5, 2011, http://www.washingtonpost.com/wp-dyn/content/article/2011/02/05/AR2011020500207.html.
5. Ibid.
6. https://www.politico.com/magazine/story/2014/05/nra-guns-second-amendment-106856

Chapter 22

1. http://www.nbcnews.com/id/35470011/ns/business-local_business/t/clarks-american-story-wealth-scandal-mystery/
2. https://mtstandard.com/opinion/columnists/one-of-montana-s-unsung-heroes-fred-whiteside-took-on/article_7fe8e437-c7f2-5c02-9f2f-2145778ca2f2.html
3. https://flatheadbeacon.com/2010/01/06/court-ruling-could-impact-montanas-campaign-finance-laws/
4. https://www.supremecourt.gov/opinions/09pdf/08-205.pdf, 45.
5. https://www.alternet.org/human-rights/thom-hartmann-corruption-new-normal-american-politics
6. https://www.fec.gov/updates/american-tradition-partnership-inc-v-bullock/
7. https://www.nytimes.com/interactive/2017/10/04/opinion/thoughts-prayers-nra-funding-senators.html
8. https://www.law.cornell.edu/supct/html/08-205.ZX.html

Chapter 23

1. https://www.nytimes.com/2001/11/12/us/examining-vote-overview-study-disputed-florida-ballots-finds-justices-did-not.html
2. https://www.washingtonpost.com/archive/opinions/2001/11/16/lessons-of-the-long-recount/6a9967f6-7741-45e3-967c-e07e24474307/?utm_term=.dcf9e9075dc2
3. https://www.youtube.com/watch?v=FJopOtIa5Xo
4. https://www.thedailybeast.com/neil-gorsuch-drives-the-supreme-court-hard-right-on-religion
5. https://www.nytimes.com/1981/04/24/opinion/in-the-nation-court-stripping.html
6. https://www.csmonitor.com/1982/0510/051005.html
7. https://www.alternet.org/right-wing/time-overthrow-kings
8. https://www.alternet.org/hartmann-radical-right-wing-supreme-court-acting-its-monarchy
9. https://time.com/5121930/koch-brothers-fall-elections/

Chapter 24

1. https://www.npr.org/templates/story/story.php?storyId=1943658
2. https://www.equalitytrust.org.uk/what-we-do-we-campaign-we-catalyse-we-co-operate
3. https://www.equalitytrust.org.uk/violence
4. https://ssaa.org.au/news-resources/research-archive/gun-murders-driven-by-poverty-and-inequality-not-gun-availability/
5. https://ssaa.org.au/assets/news-resources/research/Transnational_study_on_the_link_between_the_possession_of_a_firearm_and_the_rate_of_homicides_by_firearms.pdf
6. https://docs.google.com/spreadsheets/d/1XV4mZi3gYDgwx5PrLwqqHTUlHkwkV-6uy_yeJh3X46o/edit#gid=0
7. https://www.motherjones.com/politics/2012/07/mass-shootings-map/
8. https://library.duke.edu/digitalcollections/wlmpc_maddc02018/
9. http://www.pnas.org/content/pnas/early/2015/10/29/1518393112.full.pdf
10. https://fas.org/sgp/crs/misc/R44126.pdf
11. http://www.msnbc.com/msnbc/mass-shootings-have-become-more-frequent-the-1970s
12. https://news.northwestern.edu/stories/2017/01/shootings-us-schools-link-unemployment

Chapter 25

1. https://www.nytimes.com/2013/01/06/sunday-review/more-guns-more-killing.html
2. Ibid.

Chapter 26

1. https://www.govinfo.gov/content/pkg/USCODE-2011-title26/pdf/USCODE-2011-title26-subtitleE-chap53.pdf
2. https://en.wikipedia.org/wiki/2011_Tucson_shooting

Chapter 28

1. https://www.wired.com/story/3-d-printed-gun-blueprints-return-laws-injunction/
2. https://www.oregon.gov/ODOT/Forms/DMV/6511.pdf

Chapter 29

1. www.safeguntechnology.com
2. Roger Parloff, "Smart guns: They're ready. Are we?" *Fortune*, April 22, 2015, http://fortune.com/2015/04/22/smart-guns-theyre-ready-are-we/.
3. https://www.warren.senate.gov/newsroom/press-releases/senator-warren-co-sponsors-three-gun-safety-bills-advocates-for-common-sense-reforms

Chapter 30

1. https://www.washingtonian.com/2018/06/15/inside-dc-police-department-efforts-grapple-with-diversity/

Chapter 31

1. https://en.wikipedia.org/wiki/Overview_of_gun_laws_by_nation

ACKNOWLEDGMENTS

Special thanks go to Troy N. Miller, who worked with me for years as a producer and writer for the television show *The Big Picture*, which I hosted every night for seven years in Washington, DC. Troy worked hard as a researcher, sounding board, editor, and often cowriter on parts of this book, and deserves recognition for it. I fully expect Troy, a brilliant young graduate of Georgetown University, originally hailing from West Virginia, to be a senator from that state one of these days.

And to Shawn Taylor, my executive producer, and Nate Atwell, my video producer, for working so smoothly and well in bringing experts on this (and other) issues to our radio/TV show, where I can do my research for books like this right out in the world. Shawn helped with booking expert guests into our radio and TV programs, many of whom provided great information and anecdotes for this book. And Nate reintroduced me to the writings of Bobby Seale, which made their way into this book in several ways. I'm blessed to have such a great team helping me produce a daily radio and TV program, which supports my writing work.

At Berrett-Koehler Publishers, Steve Piersanti—who's the founder and big cheese there—worked with me from start to finish as both publisher and editor, a rare combination for a major publisher. It's been a labor of love for both of us, and I'm so grateful to Steve for his insights, rigor, and passion for this project.

Other people at BK have helped bring this book (and some projects associated with it) to you. They include (alphabetically): Maria Jesus Aguilo, Charlotte Ashlock, Shabnam Banerjee-McFarland, Leslie Crandell, Michael Crowley, Sean Davis, James Faani, Matt Fagaly, Sohayla Farman, Maren Fox, Kristen Frantz, Lesley Iura, Kylie Johnston, Arielle Kesweder, Anna Leinberger, Catherine Lengronne, Zoe Mackey, Neal Maillet, David Marshall, Liz McKellar, Sarah Modlin, Jose Ortega, Courtney Schonfeld, Katie Sheehan, Jeevan Sivasubramaniam (who has helped keep me sane for years), Nina Thompson, Jason VanDenEng, Johanna Vondeling (who edited several of my previous books so brilliantly), Edward Wade, Lasell Whipple, Ginger Winters, and Chloe Wong. BK is an extraordinary publishing company, and it's been an honor to have them publish my books for almost two decades.

They also provided a brilliant final editor for the book, Elissa Rabellino, who did a great job smoothing the text and fact-checking.

Bill Gladstone, my agent for over two decades, helped make this book—and the series of which this book is hopefully the first—possible. Bill is truly one of the best in the business.

And, as always, my best sounding board, editor, and collector of epigraphs is my wife, Louise. Without her, in all probability none of my books would have ever seen the light of day.

INDEX

ABOUT THE AUTHOR

Thom takes aim at the modern gun culture.

Thom Hartmann is the four-time Project Censored Award-winning, *New York Times* best-selling author of 25 books currently in print in over a dozen languages on five continents in the fields of psychiatry, ecology, politics, and economics, and the number one progressive talk show host in the United States.

His daily three-hour radio/TV show is syndicated on commercial radio stations nationwide, on nonprofit and community stations nationwide, in Europe and Africa by Pacifica, across the entire North American continent on SiriusXM Satellite radio, on its own YouTube channel, via podcast, worldwide through the US American Forces Network, and through the Thom Hartmann app in the App Store and for Android. The show is also simulcast as TV in real time into more than

60 million US homes by the Free Speech TV Network on Dish Network, DirectTV, and cable TV systems nationwide.

Thom has helped set up hospitals, famine relief programs, schools, and refugee centers in India, Uganda, Australia, Colombia, Russia, and the United States. Formerly rostered with the State of Vermont as a psychotherapist, founder of the Michigan Healing Arts Center, and licensed as an NLP trainer by Richard Bandler, he was the originator of the revolutionary "hunter-farmer hypothesis" to understand attention deficit hyperactivity disorder (ADHD).

In the field of environmentalism, Thom has cowritten and costarred in four documentaries with Leonardo DiCaprio and is also featured in his documentary theatrical releases *The 11th Hour* and *Ice on Fire*. Thom's book *The Last Hours of Ancient Sunlight*, about the end of the age of oil and the inspiration for *The 11th Hour*, is an international best seller and used as a textbook in many schools.

One of the things that fascinate him the most is how often hidden histories have shaped—or been obscured in an attempt to reshape—modern issues and events that are so often taken for granted, while completely missing the historical context. Thom's father, Carl Hartmann, wanted to be a professor of history, but his college education was interrupted in 1950 when his wife, Jean, became pregnant with Thom.

Carl spent most of the rest of his working life as the office manager and occasional lathe operator for a tool-and-die shop in Lansing, Michigan, but nonetheless collected more than 20,000 books, at least 3,000 of them histories or history textbooks, that became the walls and corridors of young Thom's basement bedroom. Carl's enthusiasm for and fascination with history—particularly largely unknown histories that nonetheless changed the world—is carried on in Thom's life and work.

The Hidden History of Guns and the Second Amendment was particularly intriguing for Thom to research and write. He got his first cap gun around age five and his first BB gun around eight. Although he tries to minimize the neurologically destructive effects of the lead dust that sprays into the air when guns are shot, he's enjoyed target and skeet shooting throughout his life and regularly engages in target-shooting competition with one of his brothers, who has a nice collection of handguns and a shooting range in his rural backyard.

Thom currently lives with his wife of 48 years, Louise, and their two dogs and three cats, on the Columbia River in Portland, Oregon. They're the parents of three adult children.

BOOKS BY THOM HARTMANN

Also in the Hidden History series

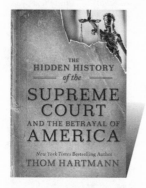

This volume of Thom Hartmann's explosive series of hidden histories critiques the omnipotent Supreme Court and offers pathways toward returning power to the people. Taking his typically in-depth, historically informed view, Hartmann asks, *What if the Supreme Court didn't have the power to strike down laws?* According to the Constitution, it doesn't. From the founding of the republic until 1803, the Supreme Court was the final court of appeals, as it was always meant to be. Hartmann argues it is not the role of the Supreme Court to decide what the law is, but rather the people themselves who vote at the ballot box. America does not belong to the kings and queens of the Court; it belongs to us.

Available at bookstores and online October 1, 2019
Paperback, 192 pages, ISBN 978-1-5230-8594-1
Digital PDF, ISBN 978-1-5230-8596-5
Digital ePub, ISBN 978-1-5230-8597-2
Digital audio, ISBN 978-1-5230-8595-8

Berrett–Koehler Publishers, Inc.
www.bkconnection.com   800.929.2929

Berrett–Koehler
Publishers

Berrett-Koehler is an independent publisher dedicated to an ambitious mission: *Connecting people and ideas to create a world that works for all.*

Our publications span many formats, including print, digital, audio, and video. We also offer online resources, training, and gatherings. And we will continue expanding our products and services to advance our mission.

We believe that the solutions to the world's problems will come from all of us, working at all levels: in our society, in our organizations, and in our own lives. Our publications and resources offer pathways to creating a more just, equitable, and sustainable society. They help people make their organizations more humane, democratic, diverse, and effective (and we don't think there's any contradiction there). And they guide people in creating positive change in their own lives and aligning their personal practices with their aspirations for a better world.

And we strive to practice what we preach through what we call "The BK Way." At the core of this approach is *stewardship,* a deep sense of responsibility to administer the company for the benefit of all of our stakeholder groups, including authors, customers, employees, investors, service providers, sales partners, and the communities and environment around us. Everything we do is built around stewardship and our other core values of *quality, partnership, inclusion,* and *sustainability.*

This is why Berrett-Koehler is the first book publishing company to be both a B Corporation (a rigorous certification) and a benefit corporation (a for-profit legal status), which together require us to adhere to the highest standards for corporate, social, and environmental performance. And it is why we have instituted many pioneering practices (which you can learn about at www.bkconnection.com), including the Berrett-Koehler Constitution, the Bill of Rights and Responsibilities for BK Authors, and our unique Author Days.

We are grateful to our readers, authors, and other friends who are supporting our mission. We ask you to share with us examples of how BK publications and resources are making a difference in your lives, organizations, and communities at www.bkconnection.com/impact.

Dear reader,

Thank you for picking up this book and welcome to the worldwide BK community! You're joining a special group of people who have come together to create positive change in their lives, organizations, and communities.

What's BK all about?

Our mission is to connect people and ideas to create a world that works for all.

Why? Our communities, organizations, and lives get bogged down by old paradigms of self-interest, exclusion, hierarchy, and privilege. But we believe that can change. That's why we seek the leading experts on these challenges—and share their actionable ideas with you.

A welcome gift

To help you get started, we'd like to offer you a free copy of one of our bestselling ebooks:

www.bkconnection.com/welcome

When you claim your **free ebook,** you'll also be subscribed to our blog.

Our freshest insights

Access the best new tools and ideas for leaders at all levels on our blog at ideas.bkconnection.com.

Sincerely,

Your friends at Berrett-Koehler